Man, The Architect Of His Own Fortune-1

Get Up With Determination

AND FIGHT

By
Dr. Sahadeva dasa

B.com., FCA., AICWA., PhD
Chartered Accountant

Soul Science University Press
www.NeverLoseHeart.net

Readers interested in the subject matter of this
book are invited to correspond with the publisher at:
SoulScienceUniversity@gmail.com   +91 98490 95990
or visit DrDasa.com

First Edition: March 2015

Soul Science University Press expresses its gratitude to the
Bhaktivedanta Book Trust International (BBT), for the use of quotes by
His Divine Grace A.C.Bhaktivedanta Swami Prabhupada.

ISBN 978-93-82947-21-9

Published by:
Dr. Sahadeva dasa for Soul Science University Press

Printed by:
Rainbow Print Pack, Hyderabad

To order a copy write to purnabramhadasa@gmail.com
or buy online: Amazon.com, rlbdeshop.com

Dedicated to....

His Divine Grace A.C.Bhaktivedanta Swami Prabhupada

"*Acapalam, determination, means that one should not be agitated or frustrated in some attempt. There may be failure in some attempt, but one should not be sorry for that; he should make progress with patience and determination.*
~ *Srila Prabhupada* (Bhagavad-gita, 16.1-3 purport)

By The Same Author

Oil-Final Countdown To A Global Crisis And Its Solutions
End of Modern Civilization And Alternative Future
To Kill Cow Means To End Human Civilization
Cow And Humanity - Made For Each Other
Cows Are Cool - Love 'Em!
Let's Be Friends - A Curious, Calm Cow
Wondrous Glories of Vraja
We Feel Just Like You Do
Tsunami Of Diseases Headed Our Way - Know Your Food Before Time
  Runs Out
Cow Killing And Beef Export - The Master Plan To Turn India Into A
  Desert
Capitalism Communism And Cowism - A New Economics For The 21st
  Century
Noble Cow - Munching Grass, Looking Curious And Just Hanging Around
World - Through The Eyes Of Scriptures
To Save Time Is To Lengthen Life
Life Is Nothing But Time - Time Is Life, Life Is Time
Lost Time Is Never Found Again
Spare Us Some Carcasses - An Appeal From The Vultures
An Inch of Time Can Not Be Bought With A Mile of Gold
Cow Dung For Food Security And Survival of Human Race
Cow Dung – A Down To Earth Solution To Global Warming And
  Climate Change
Career Women - The Violence of Modern Jobs And The Lost Art of
  Home Making
Working Moms And Rise of A Lost Generation
Glories of Thy Wondrous Name
India A World Leader in Cow Killing And Beef Export - An Italian
  Did It In 10 Years
As Long As There Are Slaughterhouses, There Will Be Wars
Peak Soil – Industrial Civilization, On The Verge of Eating Itself
If Violence Must Stop, Slaughterhouses Must Close Down
Corporatocracy - You Are A Corporate Citizen, A Slave of Invisible And
  Ruthless Masters
(More information on availability on DrDasa.com)

Contents

Preface

Just like metals and minerals lying deep inside the Earth, there are vast resources lying untapped within each of us. In man's struggles at achieving any desired object, there is in reality no necessity for him to go in quest of external forces to aid him. He has within himself vast resources and powers lying untapped, or else only partially utilized. If he applies his faculties properly and intelligently, he can easily attain his desired goal.

One of the most precious of these resources is determination. That's the unmined gold waiting to be tapped. Great personalities who perform uncommon feats, tap into these latent resources. Purpose of this book is to help you do that and light up your soul.

Scientists estimate that the average person has conscious control of about 10% of his mental powers, while the rest lie hidden like the bulk of an iceberg floating beneath the surface.

Without firm determination, your life is like a rudderless ship, tossing and turning in the ocean of material existence. So many people just drift aimlessly in their lives not knowing what they want or where they want to be. They can learn from a postage stamp whose usefulness consists in the ability to stick to one thing till it gets there.

Life in this material world is not a carefree, happy-go-lucky, all-expenses-paid luxurious romp. You have to stick on and fight on. A gigantic oak you see today was in fact just a little acorn that held its ground.

This book will inspire you to never give up, no matter what.

Sahadeva dasa

Dr. Sahadeva dasa
1st March 2015
Secunderabad, India

A Note On The Book Format

This book is based on One Victory A Day™ format. The chapters are arranged date wise. A reader need not read the book serially. He can open any chapter to find something useful for the day.

According to surveys, 80% of the books bought don't get read beyond 10% of their content. They just sit in the shelves and this is especially true in recent times.

The thickness of the book acts as a deterrent and often due to lack of time, desperation grows and the book lands in the shelf.

In One Victory A Day™ format, the book need not be 'completed'. The idea is to read the chapter related to the day, and then to understand, assimilate and implement the information. That is improving life in small measures or changing life one day at a time. During the day, you can try to reflect on and implement the newfound information.

Many of the books bought are not read completely because the reader can not relate the information to his or her life. Purpose of knowledge is not just recreation but betterment of life. Purpose of information should be transformation. Ingesting information without assimilation is like ingesting food without digestion.

To scale a highrise, you go up one step at a time. To finish your meal, you eat one morsel at a time. A skyscraper is constructed one brick at a time. An ocean is nothing but an assembly of many drops. Never underestimate the power of small. A big target is easily attainable when broken down into small steps.

People who are not into reading should cultivate the habit of reading in small installments. Phenomenal achievements are made by consistent and daily practice. Good reading is as essential as clean air and water. Anything we regularly do becomes a habit.

The mind's garden will produce whatever we sow into it. Daily we are bombarded with information, not all of which is desirable. You can counteract it by assimilating desirable information.

DETERMINATION

THE UNMINED GOLD IN YOU

Determination is a inner trait that makes you continue trying to do or achieve something that is difficult. It is sometimes referred to as 'drive' which is the resolve to get things done, to make things happen and constantly to look for better ways of doing things.

Determination is closely associated with resilience: the ability to bounce back from setbacks, rather than giving up. When the going gets tough, the tough get going! Toughness is in the soul and spirit, not in muscles.

Determination is a fire that burns in some one's soul and spurs him on. According to Benjamin Disraeli, nothing can withstand the

power of the human will if it is willing to stake its very existence to the extent of its purpose.

Vedic literatures narrate a story to explain the concept of determination.

"As for determination, one should follow the example of the sparrow who lost her eggs in the waves of the ocean. A sparrow laid her eggs on the shore of the ocean, but the big ocean carried away the eggs on its waves. The sparrow became very upset and asked the ocean to return her eggs. The ocean did not even consider her appeal. So the sparrow decided to dry up the ocean. She began to pick out the water in her small beak, and everyone laughed at her for her impossible determination. The news of her activity spread, and at last Garuda, the gigantic bird carrier of Lord Visnu, heard it. He became compassionate toward his small sister bird, and so he came to see the sparrow. Garuda was very pleased by the determination of the small sparrow, and he promised to help. Thus Garuda at once asked the ocean to return her eggs lest he himself take up the work of the sparrow. The ocean was frightened at this, and returned the eggs. Thus the sparrow became happy by the grace of Garuda."[1]

Paulo Coelho says, "When a person really desires something, all the universe conspires to help that person to realize his dream."

Bhagavad Gita, which is set in a narrative framework of a dialogue between Pandava

"AS I WAS SAYING, WITH THIS PRODUCT...."

prince Arjuna and his guide and charioteer Krishna, divides
determination in three broad categories:

dhrtya yaya dharayate
manah-pranendriya-kriyah
yogenavyabhicarinya
dhrtih sa partha sattviki

O son of Prtha, that determination which is unbreakable, which
is sustained with steadfastness by yoga practice, and which thus
controls the activities of the mind, life and senses is determination
in the mode of goodness.

yaya tu dharma-kamarthan
dhrtya dharayate 'rjuna
prasangena phalakanksi
dhrtih sa partha rajasi

But that determination by which one holds fast to fruitive results
in religion, economic development and sense gratification is of the
nature of passion, O Arjuna.

yaya svapnam bhayam sokam
visadam madam eva ca
na vimuncati durmedha
dhrtih sa partha tamasi

And that determination which cannot go beyond dreaming,
fearfulness, lamentation, moroseness and illusion -- such unintelligent
determination, O son of Prtha, is in the mode of darkness.

(Bhagavad-gita 18.33-35)

Reference:
1. Bhagavad-gita, 6.24 purport, A.C.Bhaktivedanta Swami Prabhupada, BBTI.

A Country's Fate

Inspired By A Spider

R obert I, popularly known as Robert the Bruce, was King of Scots from 1306 until his death in 1329. Robert was one of the most famous warriors of his generation, and eventually led Scotland during the Wars of Scottish Independence against England. He fought successfully during his reign to regain Scotland's place as an independent nation and is today remembered in Scotland as a national hero.

It is said that in the early days of Bruce's reign he was defeated by the English and driven into exile. He was on the run - a hunted man. He sought refuge in a small dark cave and sat and watched a little spider trying to make a web.

Time and time again the spider would fall and then climb slowly back up to try again.

If at first you don't succeed - try, try again.

Finally, as the Bruce looked on, the spider managed to stick a strand of silk to the cave wall and began to weave a web. Robert the Bruce was inspired by the spider and went on to defeat the English at the Battle of Bannockburn.

The legend as it is now told was first published by Sir Walter Scott in 'Tales of a Grandfather' in 1828, more than 500 years after the Battle of Bannockburn.

Caves across Scotland and Ireland are said to be legendary cave of Bruce and the spider: the King's Cave at Drumadoon on Arran; King Robert the Bruce's Cave in Kirkpatrick Fleming near Lockerbie; Bruce's Cave - Uamh-an-Righ, Balquhidder Glen; Bruce's Cave on Rathlin Island.

LIFE LESSONS FROM A TINY ANT

Amir Timur was a Mongolian King and great great grandfather of Babur, the founder of the Mughal dynasty in India. He was born in present day Uzbekistan and he conquered nearly half the world known at that time. Amir Taimur was firm and unfaltering in every situation. This life lesson he learnt from an ant. He tells his own story as follows.

Once he was fighting a battle and was defeated. He ran away to the mountains and hid behind some rocks. Tired and hungry, while he sat there, he noticed an ant carrying a grain of rice much bigger than itself. The ant tried to climb a wall but the grain being heavier,

fell to the floor. The ant came down and picked up the grain and tried to climb again. Again the grain slipped from its grip and again it came down to pick it up.

This process went on for hours and finally after 33 unsuccessful attempts, the ant succeeded in taking the grain up the wall. This was a life changing experience for the king.

He said to himself: "O' Taimur! You are by no means inferior to an ant. Arise and get back to work." So heartened, he went about collecting his run-away soldiers. He rebuilt his army, fought yet another battle and won. Thereafter one success after another came to him. He had learnt not to give up under any circumstances.

Constant effort is the key to success. Ants know this. They teach us not to despair.

Source:
Tales of a Grandfather, Stories from the History of Scotland Vol. I
Robert The Bruce. Publisher: Heinemann.
King Robert the Bruce By A. F. Murison
Education Scotland, Govt. of UK, Foghlam Alba
CII Youth Foundation, South African National Quraan Committee (SANQC)

klaibyam ma sma gamah partha
naitat tvayy upapadyate
ksudram hrdaya-daurbalyam
tyaktvottistha parantapa

O son of Prtha, do not yield to this degrading impotence. It does not become you. Give up such petty weakness of heart and arise, O chastiser of the enemy.
~ Bhagavad-gita 2.3

INJURED AND LYING ON THE ROAD

CHINESE STUDENT LEARNS 107 ENGLISH WORDS

WHILE WAITING FOR MEDICS TO ARRIVE

When it comes to being determined, one particular Chinese student is difficult to surpass.

Despite suffering painful injuries in a road accident in China's capital Beijing, Wang Dafan wasted no precious time while waiting for medics to arrive.

'We couldn't believe it when we got there,' said a police spokesman. 'She was obviously in pain but she was using an electronic dictionary to memorise English words for her university lessons.

'She said the accident had reminded her life was too short, and education too important, to waste time on worrying about other things.'

The 18-year-old girl was knocked off her bike by a car as she was on her way to a tutorial.

Having checked out that she would survive, she reached into her bag for the electronic gizmo while still sprawled on the ground, and set about learning 107 new English words in the time it took for an ambulance to arrive to treat injuries to her legs, head and arms.

Wang, a bright spark who has won lots of scholarships and academic prizes in her time, said: 'I was in pain but the study kept

Accident victim Wang Dafan is pictured learning new English words as she waits for an ambulance to arrive. She learnt 107 words by the time paramedics arrived

my mind off feeling hurt. I think that we are all on this earth for such a short time that we owe it to our family, friends and each others to become the best that we can be.'

'I found that studying the English words was a great help and soothed my pain.'

She is currently a student at Capital Normal University in Beijing and hopes to continue her studies at Oxford or Cambridge in the future and plans for a career in academia.

Source
Ted Thornhill, The Daily Mail, 6 May 2014
The Guardian, Tom Mctague, 12 June 2014
Beijing Times, Robert Wang Hue, 5 May 2014

matra-sparsas tu kaunteya
sitosna-sukha-duhkha-dah
agamapayino 'nityas
tams titiksasva bharata
O son of Kunti, the nonpermanent appearance of happiness and
distress, and their disappearance in due course, are like the appearance
and disappearance of winter and summer seasons. They arise from sense
perception, O scion of Bharata, and one must learn to tolerate them without
being disturbed.
  ~ Bhagavad-gita 2.14

WRITING A BOOK

BY BLINKING ONE EYELID

Jean-Dominique Bauby was a well-known French journalist, author and editor of the French fashion magazine Elle. He had two children with his wife, Sylvie de la Rochefoucauld.

On 8 December 1995 at the age of 43, Bauby suffered a massive stroke. When he woke up twenty days later, he found he was entirely speechless; he could only blink his left eyelid. Called locked-in syndrome, this is a condition wherein the mental faculties remain intact but most of the body is paralyzed. In Bauby's case his mouth, arms, and legs were paralyzed, and he lost 27 kilograms (60 lb) in the first 20 weeks after his stroke.

Despite his condition, he wrote the book The Diving Bell and the Butterfly by blinking when the correct letter was reached by a person slowly reciting the alphabet over and over again using a system called partner-assisted scanning. Bauby composed and edited the book entirely in his head, and dictated it one letter at a time.

To make dictation more efficient, Bauby's interlocutor, Claude Mendibil, listed the letters in accordance with their frequency in the French language. He tells how he would mentally write, edit and rewrite his sentences before communicating them to his therapist.

The book was published in France on 7 March 1997. Bauby died suddenly from pneumonia two days after the publication of his book, and is buried in a family grave at the Père-Lachaise cemetery in Paris, France.

In 2007, painter-director Julian Schnabel released a film version of The Diving Bell and the Butterfly. Critically acclaimed, the film received many awards and nominations including the Best Director Prize at Cannes Film Festival and the Golden Globe Award for Best Foreign Language Film & Best Director, as well as 4 Academy Award nominations.

MAKING A CHOICE

"My diving bell becomes less oppressive, and my mind takes flight like a butterfly. There is so much to do. You can wander off in space or in time, set out for Tierra del Fuego or for King Midas's court" –Jean-Dominique Bauby

The above quote from Jean-Dominique speaks volumes about his character and his ability to overcome adversity. Jean-Dominique had a choice to make: He could either lay there and play the part of a vegetable or accept his situation and try to make some good of it. Fortunately to inspire us, he chose the latter. Using only his mind, he was free to wander the world, visit with friends or imagine himself in another time. With a blink of an eye, he wrote a book. What is

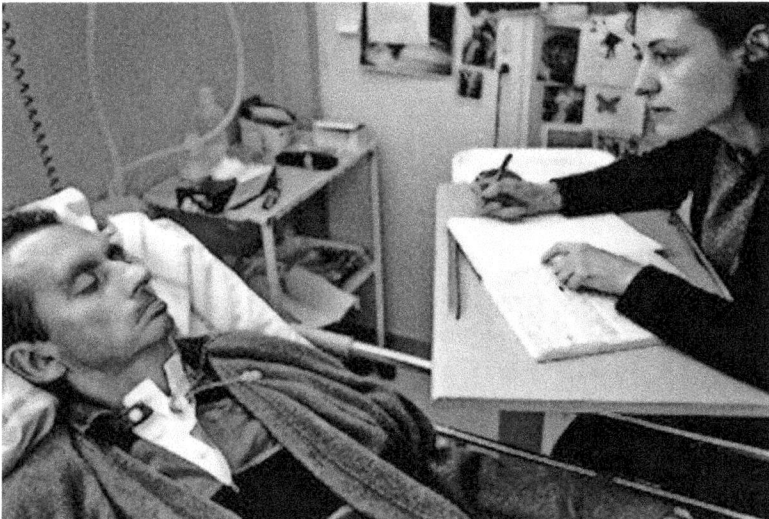

it that makes some people "overcome" adversity, while others never really seem to recover?

Source

Wikipedia, Boyles, Denis (10 October 2003). "Pre-Mortuarial Medicine". National Review Online. Archived from the original on 7 April 2005. Retrieved 4 May 2014.

Mallon, Thomas (15 June 1997). "In the Blink of an Eye". New York Times. Retrieved 4 May 2014.

Leslie Sowers Staff (20 July 1999). "`Locked-in' quadriplegic shares life". Houston Chronicle. Archived from the original on 15 October 2012. Retrieved 4 May 2014.

Bauby, Jean-Dominique (23 June 1998). The Diving Bell and the Butterfly: A Memoir of Life in Death. Knopf Doubleday Publishing Group.

Thomas, Rebecca (8 February 2008). "Diving Bell movie's fly-away success". BBC. Retrieved 4 May 2014.

Freireich, Paul (26 April 1998). "Q and A". New York Times.

Arnold, Beth (23 February 2008). "The truth about "The Diving Bell and the Butterfly"". Salon.com.

Di Giovanni, Janine (29 November 2008). "The real love story behind The Diving Bell and the Butterfly". The Guardian.

Why I am writing so many books? Not a single moment waste. If you want to become successful in Krsna consciousness, don't lose even a single moment. That should be the first determination. Avyartha-kalatvam [Cc. Madhya 23.18-19], Rupa Gosvami says. Don't go on increasing sleeping, eating, mating. These are all material necessities. If you increase these things, then you cannot make any progress in spiritual life.

~ Srila Prabhupada (Lecture, Srimad-Bhagavatam 1.16.24 -- Hawaii, January 20, 1974)

A Fighter

With A Resolve of Steel

In the epic Mahabharata, Bhisma (or Devavrata) was the eighth son of Kuru King Shantanu, who was blessed with wish-long life and had sworn to serve the ruling Kuru king. An unparalleled archer and warrior, he once fought his own guru the mighty Parasurama and defeated him. He also handed down the Vishnu Sahasranama to Yudhisthira when he was on his death bed (of arrows) in the battlefield of Kurukshetra.

Bhisma literally means He of the terrible oath, referring to his vow of lifelong celibacy. Originally named Devavrata, he became known as Bhisma after he took the bhishama pratigya ('terrible oath') — the vow of lifelong celibacy and of service to whomever sat on the throne of his father (the throne of Hastinapur).

He took this oath so that his father, Shantanu could marry a fisherwoman Satyavati — Satyavati's father had refused to give his daughter's hand to Shantanu on the grounds that his daughter's children would never be rulers. This made Shantanu despondent, and upon discovering the reason for his father's despondency, Devavrata sought out the girl's father and promised him that he would never stake a claim to the throne, implying that the child born to Shantanu and Satyavati would become the ruler after Shantanu.

At this, Satyavati's father retorted that even if Devavrata gave up his claim to the throne, his (Devavrata's) children would still claim the throne. Devavrata then took the vow of lifelong celibacy, thus sacrificing his 'crown-prince' title and denying himself the pleasures of family life. This gave him immediate recognition among the demigods.

His father granted him the boon of Ichcha Mrityu (control over his own death — he could choose the time of his death.

Bhisma's step-brothers, Chitrangad and Vichitravirya died heirless and mother Satyavati requested Bhisma to revive the lineage.

Following narration is found in Adi parva of Mahabharata, chapter 103:

'The unfortunate Satyavati then became plunged in grief on account of her son. And after performing with her daughters-in-law the funeral rites of the deceased, consoled, as best she could, her weeping daughters-in-law and Bhisma, that foremost of all wielders of weapons. And turning her eyes to religion, and to the paternal and maternal lines (of the Kurus), she addressed Bhisma and said :

'The funeral cake, the achievements, and the perpetuation of the line of the virtuous and celebrated Santanu of Kuru's race, all now depend on thee. As the attainment of heaven is inseparable from good deeds, as long life is inseparable from truth and faith, so is virtue inseparable from thee. O virtuous one, thou art well-acquainted, in detail and in the abstract, with the dictates of virtue, with various Srutis, and with

all the branches of the Vedas; know very well that thou art equal unto Sukra and Angiras as regards firmness in virtue, knowledge of the particular customs of families, and readiness of inventions under difficulties. Therefore, O foremost of virtuous men, relying on thee greatly, I shall appoint thee in a certain matter. Hearing me, it behoveth thee to do my bidding. O bull among men, my son and thy brother, endowed with energy and dear unto thee, hath gone childless to heaven while still a boy. These wives of thy brother, the amiable daughters of the ruler of Kasi, possessing beauty and youth, have become desirous of children. Therefore, O thou of mighty arms, at my command, raise offspring on them for the perpetuation of our line. It behoveth thee to guard virtue against loss. Install thyself on the throne and rule the kingdom of the Bharatas. Wed thou duly a wife. Plunge not thy ancestors into hell.'

'Thus addressed by his mother and friends and relatives, that oppressor of foes, the virtuous Bhisma, gave this reply conformable to the dictates of virtue:

asaṁśayam paro dharmas tvayā mātar udāhṛtaḥ
tvam apatyam prati ca me pratijñām vettha vai parām
'O mother, what thou sayest is certainly sanctioned by virtue. But thou knowest what my vow is in the matter of begetting children.'

jānāsi ca yathāvvṛttham śulka hetos tvad antare
sa satyavati satyam te pratijānāmy aham punaḥ
'Thou knowest also all that transpired in connection with thy dowry. O Satyavati, I repeat the pledge I once gave!'

parityajeyam trailokyam rājyam devesu vā punaḥ
yad vāpy adhikam etābhyām na tu satyam katham cana
'I would renounce three worlds, the empire of heaven, anything that may be greater than that, but truth I would never renounce.'

tyajec ca pṛthivī gandham āpaś ca rasam ātmanaḥ
jyotis tathā tyajed rūpam vāyuḥ sparśagunam tyajet
'The earth may renounce its scent, water may renounce its moisture, light may renounce its attribute of exhibiting forms, air may renounce its attribute of touch.'

prabhām samutsrjed arko dhūmaketus tathosnatām
tyajec chabdam athākāśah somah śītāmśutām tyajet
vikramam vrtrahā jahyād dharmam jahyāc ca dharmarāt
na tv aham satyam utsrastum vyavaseyam katham cana

'The sun may renounce his glory, fire, its heat, the moon, his cooling rays, space, its capacity of generating sound, Indra the slayer of Vritra, his prowess, Yamaraja the god of justice, his impartiality; but I cannot renounce truth.'

Source

"Bhishma". Encyclopedia for Epics of Ancient India.

Vyasa, Krishna-Dwaipayana; Ganguli, Kisari Mohan (1883–1896). The Mahabharata. Sacred Texts.

Kisari Mohan Ganguli. "SECTION CLXXXIX". The Mahabharata, Book 5: Udyoga Parva. Sacred-texts.com.

The Mahabharata in Sanskrit, Book 1, Chapter 97, Sacred-texts.

sauryam tejo dhrtir daksyam
yuddhe capy apalayanam
danam isvara-bhavas ca
ksatram karma svabhava-jam

Heroism, power, determination, resourcefulness, courage in battle, generosity and leadership are the natural qualities of work for the ksatriyas.

~Bhagavad-gita 18.43

EVERY OBSTACLE

PRESENTS AN OPPORTUNITY

In ancient times, a king had a boulder placed on a roadway. Then he hid himself and watched to see if anyone would remove the huge rock. Some of the king's wealthiest merchants and courtiers came by and simply walked around it.

Many loudly blamed the king for not keeping the roads clear, but none did anything about getting the big stone out of the way. Then a peasant came along carrying a load of vegetables. On approaching the boulder, the peasant laid down his burden and tried to move the stone to the side of the road. After much pushing and straining, he finally succeeded. As the peasant picked up his load of vegetables, he

noticed a purse lying in the road where the boulder had been. The purse contained many gold coins and a note from the king indicating that the gold was for the person who removed the boulder from the roadway. The peasant learned what many others never understand.

Every obstacle presents an opportunity to improve one's condition.

Reference

R. W. Hamilton, E. K. Vyhmeister, The Good E-Mails,

Lyndall Briggs, Gary Green, Soul Purpose: Self Development Stories, Quotes and Poems

Stanley D. Prueitt, Unleash the Leader

So kecit. Kecit means this determination is very difficult. Therefore it has been said here, kecit, "somebody," not all. Not all can get that determination. But everyone can get determination, provided he likes it. It is not that determination is monopolized by a certain man. Anyone who determines that "I shall simply serve Krsna," that simple determination will save him. Kevalaya bhaktya.

~ Srila Prabhupada (Lecture, Srimad-Bhagavatam 6.1.15 -- Honolulu, May 15, 1976)

Struggle

Sometimes You Need It

A man found a cocoon of a butterfly. One day a small opening appeared. He sat and watched the butterfly for several hours as it struggled to force its body through that little hole. Then it seemed to stop making any progress. It appeared as if it had gotten as far as it could, and it could go no further.

So the man decided to help the butterfly. He took a pair of scissors and snipped off the remaining bit of the cocoon.

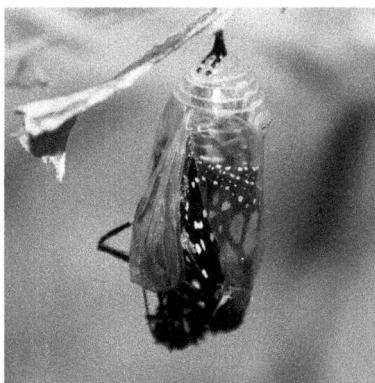

The butterfly then emerged easily. But it had a swollen body and small, shriveled wings.

The man continued to watch the butterfly because he expected that, at any moment, the wings would enlarge and expand to be able to support the body, which would contract in time.

Neither happened! In fact, the butterfly spent the rest of its life crawling around with a swollen body and shriveled wings. It never was able to fly.

What the man, in his kindness and haste, did not understand was that the restricting cocoon and the struggle required for the butterfly to get through the tiny opening were God's way of forcing fluid from the body of the butterfly into its wings so that it would be ready for flight once it achieved its freedom from the cocoon.

Sometimes struggles are exactly what we need in our lives. If God allowed us to go through our lives without any obstacles, it would cripple us.

We would not be as strong as what we could have been. We could never fly!

Reference

Thomas Pafe, The Religion of Love: A Manual to Guide You on the Path to Enlightenment, iUniverse

Raksha Bharadia, Roots And Wings, Rupa Publications

Dan Miller, 48 Days to the Work You Love: An Interactive Study, B&H Publishing Group.

mamaivamso jiva-loke
jiva-bhutah sanatanah
manah-sasthanindriyani
prakrti-sthani karsati
The living entities in this conditioned world are My eternal fragmental parts. Due to conditioned life, they are struggling very hard with the six senses, which include the mind.
~ Bhagavad-gita 15.7

STORY OF AN INCREDIBLE VOYAGE

RIVEN WITH TRAGEDY, INSANITY AND UNIMAGINABLE HARDSHIP

A RECORD-BREAKING FEAT OF HUMAN SURVIVAL, PUSHED TO THE OUTERMOST LIMITS OF HUMAN ENDURANCE

José Alvarenga is a Salvadoran man who was found on 30 January 2014, aged 36, in the Marshall Islands, after drifting for 14 months and 6,500 miles on a tiny boat lost in the Pacific Ocean. He is reported to have survived on a diet of raw fish, turtles, small birds, sharks, and rainwater. He swam to shore on January 30. Two locals, found him naked, clutching a knife and shouting in Spanish. He was treated in a hospital before flying to his family home in El Salvador.

IT STARTED LIKE ANY OTHER DAY

The day everything changed, November 17, 2012, had started much like any other in Costa Azul, the south-west Mexican village where he lived in a wooden shack provided by the boss of his fishing fleet.

Rising early after swigging a six-pack of Corona beers in the local beach-bar, he was eager to go out fishing to earn some Christmas money, but needed a stand-in partner because his regular engine operator, Ray Perez, was on bail for some drunken crime and had to report to the police.

Wandering along the shore, he happened upon Ezequiel, whom he didn't know. 'You want to come out fishing?' he asked.

The young greenhorn admitted he had only ventured onto the open sea a handful times, always with his brothers, but he was eager to learn, so they teamed up.

Hearing a storm was forecast, they delayed their departure until 9am. Then Jose heard that others in the fleet had felt it safe enough to go out, so they coiled their 4-mile line with its 700 hooks into the hold, cranked up the Yamaha engine, and puttered down the lagoon leading to the Pacific.

IT WAS JUST ANOTHER VOYAGE

Jose had packed a change of clothes and more than enough food for the single day and night he planned to be away: fried liver and rice, and some lemons, onions and salt to make the Mexican dish ceviche, plus 20 litres of water. Ezequiel would share.

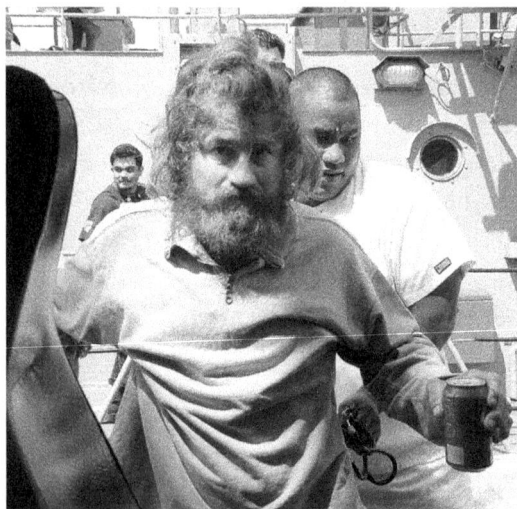

Safe! The first picture of Jose Alvarenga when he was brought to the mainland in the Marshall Islands, bedraggled, dazed and frail in February.

The open boat also carried an ice-packed cooling box for the fish, two-way radio and GPS, three plastic petrol canisters, three knives of varying lengths for gutting and slicing, a sheet to sleep under, and some bleach bottles to serve as buoys for the fishing line.

Jose wore his usual outfit – canvas pants, a vest, a broad-brimmed hat and a ski-mask to protect his face from the scorching sun. Ezequiel sported shorts, T-shirts and a pirate-style T-shirt with skull-and-crossbones. He had no hat, so Jose lent him one.

'Hey kid, do you reckon you can handle being at sea for 24 hours?' Jose remarked with prophetic irony as they left.

'Sure I can,' came the indignant response.

Though Jose was forced to navigate and do most of the fishing, because Ezequiel was inexperienced, the trip exceeded all expectations.

By nightfall the boat was laden with 200-pounds of hammerhead shark and 800-pounds of gilthead sea-bream: a bumper catch.

They had stopped the engine some 40 miles offshore, and were resting up ready to return to Costa Azul at first light when, from nowhere, the storm erupted.

WHEN THE UNEXPECTED HAPPENS

It began with thunder and a freshening of 'El Norte' – the unpredictable north wind that has claimed so many Central American fishermen's lives – but soon became an unrelenting gale that whipped the sea into a cauldron the like of which Jose had never witnessed.

As the boat pitched and tossed, Ezequiel froze with panic, Jose says candidly. 'He was crying and crying, and curled into a ball, covering head in his hands.

'I urged him to help by throwing the catch overboard to lessen our weight, but he couldn't so I had to do it all by myself. It might sound harsh, but it's the truth.

> *Rakhe krsna mare ke mare krsna rakhe ke.* "He whom Krsna protects, no one can kill, but if Krsna wants to kill someone, no one can give him protection." For example, suppose a very rich man is suffering from disease. He may have a first-class physician, medicine, and hospital available for him, but still he may die. This means that Krsna desired, "This man must die." Therefore, the so-called protective methods we have devised will be useless if Krsna does not desire us to live. The demon Ravana was very powerful, but when Krsna in the form of Lord Ramacandra desired to kill him, no one could protect him. Therefore, if God wants to kill someone, no one can give him protection, and if God wants to protect someone, no one can kill him.
> ~ Srila Prabhupada (Teaching of Queen Kunti 7: Dangerous Encounters)

'I had been on a survival course and followed my training. First I tied myself to the boat with a rope. Then I punctured holes in the empty gas canisters, lashed them to the boat and hurled them overboard to break the waves and act as stabilisers. I cut the bleach bottles in half and used them to bale the water.

'If I hadn't done all that we'd surely have sunk and drowned. The storm raged on four days, and then, suddenly, the sea was as flat as a road again.

'We had lost everything apart from the smallest knife, my ski-mask, which I later used to patch holes in my clothes using fish bones as needles and sinew from birds as thread, the bleach bottles, in which I collected rainwater, and the cooler box, which served as a sun-shade in the daytime and a shield from the cold winds at night.

'The radio and GPS had gone and the engine had broken, and I knew instinctively that we had drifted too far from the land to have any chance of being found; maybe 200 miles or more.

'I had this strange buzzing in my ears, which seemed to be something to do with the change of pressure caused by the huge depth of the water.

'And I have never known such silence, such emptiness. In every direction I looked there was…just nothing. It is impossible to explain how it really feels to be trapped, at God's mercy, in such a never-ending void.'

The material world is full of dangers (padam padam yad vipadam [SB 10.14.58]). For example, if one is on the ocean one may have a very strong ship, but that ship can never be safe; because one is at sea, at any time there may be dangers. The Titanic was safe, but on its first voyage it sank, and many important men lost their lives. So danger there must be, because we are in a dangerous position. This material world itself is dangerous. Therefore, our business now should be to cross over this sea of danger as soon as possible.

~ Srila Prabhupada (Teaching of Queen Kunti 8: Let There Be Calamities)

Jose marked the passing days by the size of the moon, a method his grandfather had taught him as a boy. He guessed they were drifting roughly south-west by the position of the sun, but with his limited geographical knowledge had no idea when, if ever, they might find land.

UTTERLY DESOLATE, IN THE VAST BLUE YONDER

For the first several days he and Ezekiel did not eat anything and drank only rainwater, Jose said, as they were too awestruck even to contemplate trying to catch sea-creatures or gather rainwater.

Gradually, however, Jose said it became evident that they were coping with their predicament in very different ways.

Jose began to see it as a battle for survival and summoned all his powers, mental and physical, to stay alive.

With Crusoe-esque ingenuity, he learned to scoop fish from the water with his cupped hands, catch upturned

Shelter: Jose and Ezequiel spent nights in each other's arms to provide each other with comfort and warmth

turtles unawares as they bobbed their heads for food, and trap seagulls by their feet as they perched on the boat, ripping off their wings to render them incapable of escape.

And somehow he forced himself to eat these disgustingly unpalatable creatures, covering his nose to avoid retching as he did so.

When, rarely, it rained, he sipped water gathered in the bleach bottles; during droughts he drank his own urine and sweet, sticky turtle blood. He was, as he says 'prepared to do whatever it took.'

But to Ezekiel, Jose said, hope was futile and death was inevitable: it was only a matter of how and when it would come to claim them.

For the first month, Jose says, his friend tried his hardest. He would engage in fleeting conversations, confiding to Jose that he had a girlfriend, with whom he had a troubled relationship because she hated his drinking. He also said she was pregnant.

During that first month, Ezequiel ate a little raw fish - it took him half a day to swallow his first mouthful.

'I used to cut it into small pieces and feed it to him like you would do with a little child,' Jose recalls.

As the days went by and it became clear that no-one would find them, however, Ezequiel stopped eating and drinking altogether. And slowly, excruciatingly, Jose watched his mind unravel.

'He started saying crazy things, like asking me to go and buy him food from the grocery store,' Jose remembers, shaking his head sadly.

'He would stare out to sea and say: 'Look, over there, that store is selling fresh mangos and tortillas – you have to go and get us some!'

'I would try to calm him down and humour him. I'd say: "Yes, I see the store, but it's closed now. It will be open later – I'll go and get you some mangos then."'

Even in this delusional state, however, in Ezequiel he had a companion; another soul with whom to share the fear and loneliness, and provide some comfort when darkness descended.

---

balasya neha saranam pitarau nrsimha
nartasya cagadam udanvati majjato nauh
taptasya tat-pratividhir ya ihanjasestas
tavad vibho tanu-bhrtam tvad-upeksitanam
My Lord Nrsimha-deva, O Supreme, because of a bodily conception of life, embodied souls neglected and not cared for by You cannot do anything for their betterment. Whatever remedies they accept, although perhaps temporarily beneficial, are certainly impermanent. For example, a father and mother cannot protect their child, a physician and medicine cannot relieve a suffering patient, and a boat on the ocean cannot protect a drowning man.
~ Srimad Bhagavatam 7.9.19

SPIRITUAL EXPERIENCE

About a month before Ezequiel died, Jose – who previously had no time for religion - claims to have had a powerful spiritual experience.

'I was laying in the boat one night, praying for God to send an angel to protect us, when this figure rose up before me. I thought at first it was a woman, because 'she' had a beautiful, high-pitched laugh and wore long white robes, but I never saw her face because it was shrouded by a hood.

'Somehow I wasn't afraid, But I thought I must be hallucinating and didn't want to appear crazy, so I said nothing to Ezequiel.

'The next night, the same thing happened so I thought the figure

Agony: Curled up in the boat's cooler box without so much as a sheet to protect him from the chill night winds, Jose rarely slept before he was awakened by some unimaginable nightmare

So our counteracting methods, even though they are very efficient, still, unless they are sanctioned by God, they will not be effective. There are many such examples. Some years ago, perhaps you know, in America, they started one very strong and stout ship. It was known... I think it was named Titanic. So it was guaranteed that it will never be drowned; it was so well-built. And all the important men of America started in that ship for the first time, and after a few miles it drowned. So in spite of all scientific protection, in spite of all good brains behind the manufacturing of this Titanic ship, it was drowned.

Therefore this is a fact, that you may arrange everything very nicely, according to your best knowledge, but if God is unfavorable, then you cannot do it. Daiva. Na ca daiva param balam. Therefore it is said there is no other superior strength than daiva. One has to accept this.

~ Srila Prabhupada (Lecture, The Nectar of Devotion -- Bombay, December 28, 1972)

must be real and I started to tell Ezequiel what I'd seen. "Oh, I already know what you're going to ask me," he said. "Did I see the woman in white who came to visit us?" It turned out that Ezequiel had experienced exactly the same vision.

When Ezequiel died, maybe it was the figure in white who took

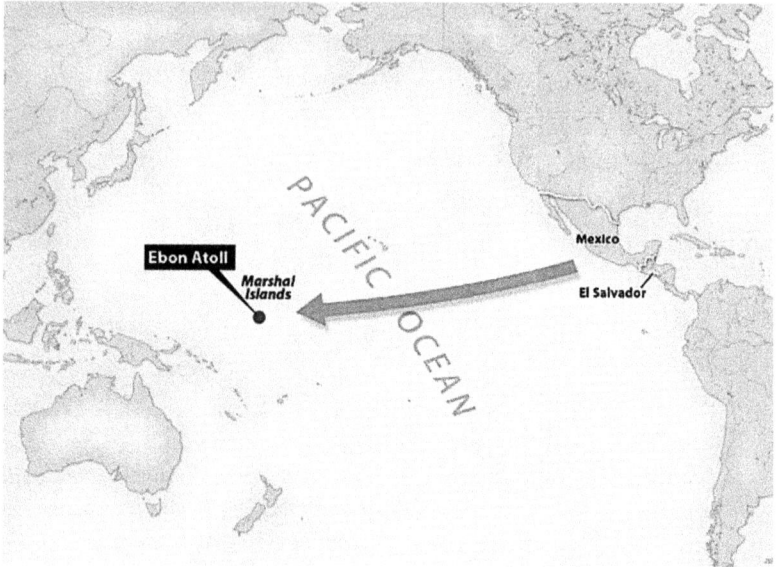

Astonishing feat: Thirteen months after heading out on a shark hunting trip from Mexico, he came ashore on the Marshall Islands, which are about 5,500 miles from where he set off

him.'

When his companion died, Jose was utterly desolate in the most remote place on earth. For the ensuing nine months he was pushed to the outermost limits of human endurance. His only companion was his unswerving faith.

NEAR, YET SO FAR

Fearing he might fail to spot the passing ship that could end his lonely torment, Jose Alvarenga would spend hour upon hour scanning the horizon for a distant funnel or a sailing mast.

Then, after drifting in the Pacific for seven months, he saw her – a big container vessel ploughing through the ocean - close enough for him to make out the huddle of crewmen standing on deck.

Barely able to contain his joy, he tore off his ragged shirt and began waving it frantically above his head, shouting for help and praising God as he did so.

Surely now he would be rescued, he thought, his heart pounding. After all, it must be obvious he was cast adrift. Why else would a tiny fishing boat be bobbing about, thousands of miles from the coast?

To his utter despair, however, the men began waving back at him, as if returning a friendly greeting, and the ship continued on its way.

Here he is pictured with his parents after he was flown home to El Salvador

'Come back you fools - you stupid cowards!' Jose bellowed as his hope of salvation chugged away. Then he sank to his knees, hammered at the hull with his fists, and wept.

Why didn't the container ship's crew come to his aid?'It's a question I often ask myself, but only they can answer,' he says bitterly.'I wonder how they live with themselves now they know my story.'

This cruel act of abandonment was among the darkest moments in the nine months he spent alone in the 24ft boat after his companion, Ezequiel Cordova, had starved to death.

'But almost every moment I spent on the ocean was dark,' he adds bleakly.'There were times when I felt my head would explode because it was so full of black thoughts.

'It was as though I had a vice clamped tightly to my temples, and all I could do was pray for it to stop. You see, there was this constant battle raging in my mind: it was God versus the Devil.

'God was telling me I must live, that my life had a purpose. The Devil was urging me to give up; that I would be better off dead.

'I would wrestle with these suicidal thoughts all the time. I couldn't imagine drowning myself - though that was the obvious way to do it - so one day I decided I'd stab myself with the fish-gutting knife I'd managed to salvage during the storm.

'I pressed the six-inch blade to my neck hard enough to feel the pressure, and I could hear the Devil's voice saying: "Go on, just do it! Why are you suffering? End it, now!"

'Then another voice spoke to me. He told me I must survive to tell the world that God does exist and he is more powerful than the Devil, and I dropped the knife.

'I'm not religious and never went to church before this happened. But I promised then that I would live a better life and do God's work if I was given the chance.

Curled up in the boat's cooler box without so much as a sheet to protect him from the chill night winds, Jose rarely slept for more than a couple of hours before he was awakened by some unimaginable nightmare.

In one recurring dream he was engulfed by great sheets of flame raining from the skies.

To maintain a sense of order and discipline, he followed a daily routine, eating three times a day and spending the rest of his time hunting, gathering rainwater, singing is favourite songs, and praying.

SOLITARY COMPANIONS

Some six months into his ordeal another welcome interlude occurred, though it began in a terrifying manner.

As he watched for passing ships, something thudded into the boat with the force of a torpedo.

Looking over the side, he saw what he feared to be a sea-monster; a bluish-grey leviathan so huge that he couldn't see its tail-fin.

The round-nosed creature – which he now believes to have been a sperm whale - could have flipped the boat over in an instant, but he quickly surmised that it had no intention of harming him.

Instead, like some magical Disney creation, it wallowed tightly alongside the wooden craft for 15 days, as if to guide him.

'He became my friend and I thought up a name for him. For some reason, I called him 'Torilio', which doesn't mean anything, and I would lean over to stroke him.

'Sometimes I fantasised about riding ashore on his back, or being carried to safety in his belly, like Jonah in the Bible. But then, one morning, I woke up and he had gone.'

Though he lived in fear of being capsized and devoured by a big sea predator, the sharks unwittingly became his allies, too.

Yama, the Lord of death appeared as a child and instructed the queens of king Suyajna who were lamenting over his dead body:

It is wonderful that these elderly women do not have a higher sense of life than we do. Indeed, we are most fortunate, for although we are children and have been left to struggle in material life, unprotected by father and mother, and although we are very weak, we have not been vanquished or eaten by ferocious animals. Thus we have a firm belief that the Supreme Personality of Godhead, who has given us protection even in the womb of the mother, will protect us everywhere.

The boy addressed the women: O weak women! Only by the will of the Supreme Personality of Godhead, who is never diminished, is the entire world created, maintained and again annihilated. This is the verdict of the Vedic knowledge. This material creation, consisting of the moving and nonmoving, is exactly like His plaything. Being the Supreme Lord, He is completely competent to destroy and protect.

Sometimes one loses his money on a public street, where everyone can see it, and yet his money is protected by destiny and not seen by others. Thus the man who lost it gets it back. On the other hand, if the Lord does not give protection, even money maintained very securely at home is lost. If the Supreme Lord gives one protection, even though one has no protector and is in the jungle, one remains alive, whereas a person well protected at home by relatives and others sometimes dies, no one being able to protect him.

~ Srimad Bhagavatam 7.2.38-40

They would sometimes trap fish against the side of the boat and if he was quick he was able to scoop them from the water before the shark clamped them in its jaws.

Attempting to escape an advancing shark, fish and squid would also jump and slither into the boat and provide him with a ready meal.

He usually had an adequate supply of protein-rich food, therefore. As it was raw and barely digestible flesh, however, he would suffer from agonizing bouts of constipation.

Since he had no fruit or vegetables and little fresh water, the miracle was that he didn't suffer other major ailments, such as scurvy.

Yet he estimates that he would have been dead within another month, at most, had the currents not carried him to the remote Ebon Atoll in the Marshall Islands where he was washed ashore.

'By then I could feel my spirit and strength ebbing away,' he says.

DELIVERANCE

He knew deliverance had finally come when, scanning the horizon one morning he spied a stand of coconut palms.

For a few minutes he feared it was another delusion. When he satisfied himself that the trees were real, his every instinct was to jump from the boat and start swimming.

Mindful of the dangers, however, he remained patient and allowed the tide to carry him ashore.

'It's a miracle! Thank God!' were the first words he uttered, as he clambered from boat and collapsed.

yam hi na vyathayanty ete
purusam purusarsabha
sama-duhkha-sukham dhiram
so 'mrtatvaya kalpate
O best among men [Arjuna], the person who is not disturbed by happiness and distress and is steady in both is certainly eligible for liberation.
~ Bhagavad-gita 2.15

He was found by kindly islanders who gave him fresh clothes and fed him rice and chunks of coconut, not realising this sudden change of diet would make him sick.

He was given food and shelter on the atoll for five days, sleeping on a straw mat on the floor of a hut - which seemed luxurious by comparison with the cooler box.

Three months later, he still seems confused on occasion and quite evidently, far more fragile than he looks at first sight.

Meanwhile, 37-year-old Jose is recovering at his parents' home in Garita Palmera. The enigmatic castaway now suffers panic-attacks if he so much as steps near the waves that crash on to the nearby beach.

And no night passes, he says, without him being haunted by nightmarish visions of the vast blue yonder.

Source

David Jones, El Salvador, The Daily Mail, 24 April 2014

Lydia Warren, The Daily Mail, 30 January 2014

Tuckman, Jo (4 February 2014). "José Salvador Alvarenga's 13 months at sea backed by fishermen and officials". The Guardian.

"Jose Salvador Alvarenga's family had given him up for dead". CBC.ca. 4 February 2014.

Walker, Brian (3 February 2014). "Castaway claims he drifted 13 months in Pacific". CNN.

Johnson, Giff (4 February 2014). "Real-Life Castaway Survived On Dreams Of Tortillas And Family". Business Insider.

Pearlman, Jonathan (4 February 2014). "Castaway's family in El Salvador rejoice at his survival". The Daily Telegraph.

Through parental care, through remedies for different kinds of disease, and through means of protection on the water, in the air, and on land, there is always an endeavor for relief from various kinds of suffering in the material world, but none of them are guaranteed measures for protection. ... Ultimately the shelter is the Lord, and one who takes shelter of the Lord is protected. This is guaranteed. ...
~ Srila Prabhupada (Titanic Disasters)

Pearlman, Jonathan (3 February 2014). "Too incredible to be true? Survivor tells of Pacific ordeal". The Daily Telegraph.

De Graaf, Mia (4 February 2014). "'I saw him alive in my dreams': Stunned mother of Pacific castaway who claimed to have spent 14 months adrift at sea wants him home as his daughter, 14, says first thing she will do is hug and kiss him". The Daily Mail.

Connor, Tracy (4 February 2014). "'Mexican fisherman shore up Marshall Islands castaway's account'". NBC News.

"Fishy Story? Details Of Castaway's Tale Adrift At Sea Confirmed But Doubts Remain". Fox News Latino. 4 February 2014.

Pearlman, Jonathan (8 February 2014). "Castaway: two Pacific islanders, a screaming naked fisherman and three omelettes". The Daily Telegraph.

"We have got experience. When I was going to New York on ship, I had no money to go by plane. So in the deep sea ocean, especially in the Atlantic Ocean, it was nothing, like a small ball, tottering like this. At any moment it can capsize. Although very big ship with very big load, but it is nothing in the sea. So there is no surety. There is no surety that because you are in a big ship you'll be saved -- no.

"In your country, it happened, say, fifty, sixty years, the Titanic. In the first voyage, everyone drowned, all big, big men. So nature's freak is so strong, that you cannot say that 'Because I have got a nice ship, I'll be saved.' No, that is not possible. Without Krsna's protection, all these counteracting measures will be all useless. Therefore teach people how to take shelter of Krsna."

~ Srila Prabhupada (A Transcendental Diary 1-9: Sri Dhama Mayapur)

THE POWER OF YOUR MIND

TO HEAL OR HARM YOU

L issa Rankin's book Mind Over Medicine is full of data scientifically proving that the mind can heal- or harm- the body. Following true story demonstrates how powerfully the mind affects our physiology.

MR. WRIGHT

As reported by Bruno Klopfer in the Journal of Projective Techniques in 1957, Dr. West was treating Mr. Wright, who had an advanced cancer called lymphosarcoma. All treatments had failed, and time was running out. Mr. Wright's neck, chest, abdomen, armpits, and groin were filled with tumors the size of oranges, his spleen and liver were enlarged, and his cancer was causing his chest to fill up with two quarts of milky fluid every day, which had to be drained in order for him to breathe. Dr. West didn't expect him to last a week.

But Mr. Wright desperately wanted to live, and he hung his hope on a promising new drug called Krebiozen. He begged his doctor to treat him with the new drug, but the drug was only being offered in clinical trials to people who were believed to have at least three months left to live. Mr. Wright was too sick to qualify.

But Mr. Wright didn't give up. Knowing the drug existed and believing the drug would be his miracle cure, he pestered his doctor

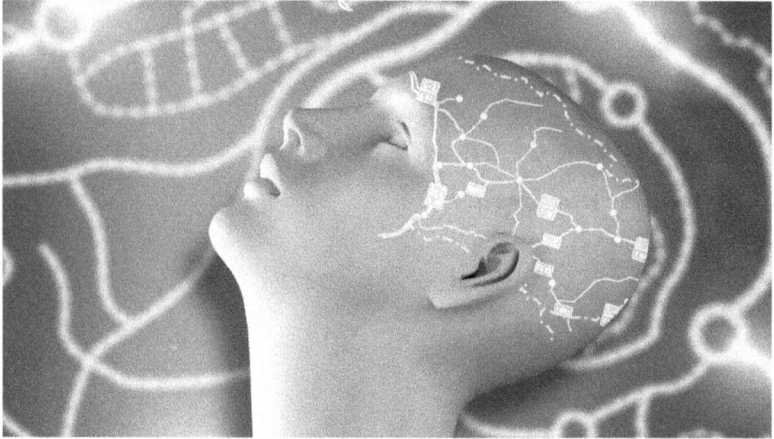

until Dr. West reluctantly gave in and injected him with Krebiozen on a Friday.

To his utter shock, the following Monday, Dr. West found his patient walking around out of bed. Mr. Wright's "tumor masses had melted like snowballs on a hot stove" and were half their original

jitatmanah prasantasya
paramatma samahitah
sitosna-sukha-duhkhesu
tatha manapamanayoh

For one who has conquered the mind, the Supersoul is already reached, for he has attained tranquillity. To such a man happiness and distress, heat and cold, honor and dishonor are all the same.

As soon as one's mind is controlled through one of the yoga systems, one should be considered to have already reached the destination. One has to abide by superior dictation. When one's mind is fixed on the superior nature, he has no alternative but to follow the dictation of the Supreme. The mind must admit some superior dictation and follow it. The effect of controlling the mind is that one automatically follows the dictation of the Paramatma, or Supersoul. Because this transcendental position is at once achieved by one who is in Krsna consciousness, the devotee of the Lord is unaffected by the dualities of material existence, namely distress and happiness, cold and heat, etc. This state is practical samadhi, or absorption in the Supreme.

~ Bhagavad-gita 6.7

size. Ten days after the first dose of Krebiozen, Mr. Wright left the hospital, apparently cancer free.

Mr. Wright was rockin' and rollin', praising Krebiozen as a miracle drug for two months until the scientific literature began reporting that Krebiozen didn't seem to be effective. Mr. Wright, who trusted what he read in the literature, fell into a deep depression, and his cancer came back.

This time, Dr. West, who genuinely wanted to help save his patient, decided to get sneaky. He told Mr. Wright—that some of the initial supplies of the drug had deteriorated during shipping, making them less effective, but that he scored a new batch of highly concentrated, ultra-pure Krebiozen, which he could give him. (Of course, this was a bold-faced lie.)

Dr. West then injected Mr. Wright with nothing but distilled water. And a seemingly miraculous thing happened—again. The tumors melted away, the fluid in his chest disappeared, and Mr. Wright was feeling great again for another two months.

Then the American Medical Association blew it by announcing that a nationwide study of Krebiozen proved that the drug was utterly

---

bandhur atmatmanas tasya
yenatmaivatmana jitah
anatmanas tu satrutve
vartetatmaiva satru-vat

For him who has conquered the mind, the mind is the best of friends; but for one who has failed to do so, his mind will remain the greatest enemy.

The purpose of practicing eightfold yoga is to control the mind in order to make it a friend in discharging the human mission. One who cannot control his mind lives always with the greatest enemy, and thus his life and its mission are spoiled. The constitutional position of the living entity is to carry out the order of the superior. As long as one's mind remains an unconquered enemy, one has to serve the dictations of lust, anger, avarice, illusion, etc. But when the mind is conquered, one voluntarily agrees to abide by the dictation of the Personality of Godhead, who is situated within the heart of everyone as Paramatma.

~ Bhagavad-gita 6.6

worthless. This time, Mr. Wright lost all faith in his treatment. His cancer came right back, and he died two days later.

Source

Lissa Rankin, MD, Stories That Will Make You Believe In the Power of Your Mind To Heal You, November 14th, 2013

Mind Over Medicine: Scientific Proof You Can Heal Yourself, By Lissa Rankin, Hay House Inc.

12 Stories To Make You Believe In The Power Of Your Mind To Heal You, The Mind Unleashed, Dec 9, 2013

PRECIOUS YOU

INVALUABLE AND PRICELESS

A well known speaker started off his seminar by holding up a $20 bill. In the room of 200, he asked, "Who would like this $20 bill?"

Hands started going up.

He said, "I am going to give this $20 to one of you but first, let me do this." He proceeded to crumple the dollar bill up.

He then asked, "Who still wants it?"

Still the hands were up in the air.

"Well," he replied, "What if I do this?" And he dropped it on the ground and started to grind it into the floor with his shoe.

He picked it up, now all crumpled and dirty. "Now who still wants it?" Still the hands went into the air.

"My friends, you have all learned a very valuable lesson. No matter what I did to the money, you still wanted it because it did not decrease in value. It was still worth $20.

Many times in our lives, we are dropped, crumpled, and ground into the dirt by the decisions we make and the circumstances that

come our way. We may feel as though we are worthless and useless.

But no matter what has happened or will happen, you will never lose your value: dirty or clean, crumpled or finely creased, you are as priceless as ever before.

People will hate you, rate you, shake you, and break you. But how strong you stand is what MAKES YOU.

-unknown

Reference

Author Unknown

Nihal Abeyasingha, Sunday Homilies: Bringing Together Exegesis and Catechesis, Dorrance Publishing.

Anthony Pereira, Oh! for Heaven's Sakes!, Volume 1, Trafford Publishing

Rollan A Roberts II, Born to Be Rich: How to Become a Money Magnet by Living Life on Purpose, Tate Publishing.

labdhva sudurlabham idam bahu-sambhavante
manusyam arthadam anityam apiha dhirah
turnam yateta na pated anu mrtyu yavan
nihsreyasaya visayah khalu sarvatah syat
"This human form of life is obtained after many, many births, and although it is not permanent, it can offer the highest benefits. Therefore a sober and intelligent man should immediately try to fulfill his mission and attain the highest profit in life before another death occurs. He should avoid sense gratification, which is available in all circumstances."
~ Srimad-Bhagavatam (11.9.29)

SHAKE IT OFF

AND STEP UP

This parable is told of a farmer who owned an old mule. The mule fell into the farmer's well. The farmer heard the mule praying or whatever mules do when they fall into wells.

After carefully assessing the situation, the farmer sympathized with the mule, but decided that neither the mule nor the well was worth the trouble of saving. Instead, he called his neighbors together, told them what had happened, and enlisted them to help haul dirt to bury the old mule in the well and put him out of his misery.

Initially the old mule was hysterical! But as the farmer and his neighbors continued shoveling and the dirt hit his back, a thought struck him. It suddenly dawned on him that every time a shovel load of dirt landed on his back, he would shake it off and step up!

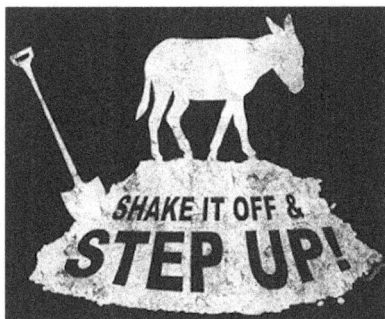

This he did, blow after blow. "Shake it off and step up… shake it off and step up… shake it off and step up!" He repeated to encourage himself. No matter how painful the blows, or how distressing the situation seemed, the old mule fought panic and just kept right on shaking it off and stepping up!

It wasn't long before the old mule, battered and exhausted, stepped triumphantly over the wall of that well! What seemed like it would bury him actually helped him ... all because of the manner in which he handled his adversity.

That's life! If we face our problems and respond to them positively, and refuse to give in to panic, bitterness, or self-pity.

Reference

Author Unknown

Dario A. Shields, Ghetto Born, God Raised: It's Not Your Setbacks, It's How You Comeback

Stephen, Moral Stories, October 14, 2008

Sharilyn A. Ross, The Spirit of Camp, Xulon Press

Doris M. Arwine, Sensitive to Listen and Willing to Obey, WestBow Press

George D. Johnson, Wisdom II, Xlibris Corporation

hato va prapsyasi svargam
jitva va bhoksyase mahim
tasmad uttistha kaunteya
yuddhaya krta-niscayah
O son of Kunti, either you will be killed on the battlefield and attain the heavenly planets, or you will conquer and enjoy the earthly kingdom. Therefore, get up with determination and fight.
~ Bhagavad-gita 2.37

WHEN YOU DECIDE TO DO SOMETHING

DEEP FROM YOUR HEART

An old man lived alone in an American town. His only son was in prison. The old man wrote a letter to his son.

Dear Son,

I am feeling pretty bad because it looks like I won't be able to plant my potato garden this year. I'm just getting too old to be digging up a garden plot. If you were here, all my troubles would be over. I know you would dig the plot for me, if you weren't in prison.

Love,

Dad

Shortly, the old man received this telegram:

'For Heaven's sake, Dad, don't dig up the garden !! That's where I buried the GUNS !!'

At 4 a.m. the next morning, a dozen FBI agents and local police officers showed up and dug up the entire garden without finding any guns.

Confused, the old man wrote another note to his son telling him what had happened, and asked him what to do next.

His son's reply was:

'Go ahead and plant your potatoes, Dad. It's the best I could do for you, from here.'

Moral: No matter where you are in the world, if you have decided to do something deep from your heart, you can do it. It is the thought that matters, not your external circumstances.

Reference:

Author Unknown

RJI, Moral Booster short story, April 1, 2013

Laura Cox, Life Is A Game, Be The Player, June 2002

Just see, a sparrow is trying to dry up the ocean. (laughs) This is called determination. Just like our Gandhi. He declared war against the Britishers. And that war is non-violent, noncooperation. You see? But the determination was there. That "I must drive away the Britishers." And he did it. And what is the weapon? Nonviolence. "All right, you fight, you kill me, I shall not attack you." You see? He became, what is that? Determined. People laughed. "Gandhi is declaring war with the Britishers, so powerful, British Empire." And actually after the Britishers lost India, they lost the whole Empire. Because that was the jewel of British Empire. They lost all the possession in the Far East, they lost possession in Egypt, they lost possession on Suez Canal, everything lost. So determination is such a nice thing.

~ Srila Prabhupada (Bhagavad-gita 6.16-24 -- Los Angeles, February 17, 1969)

STORY OF A CRIPPLE

AND HIS SHEER DETERMINATION

The little country schoolhouse was heated by an old-fashioned, pot-bellied coal stove. A little boy had the job of coming to school early each day to start the fire and warm the room before his teacher and his classmates arrived.

One morning they arrived to find the schoolhouse engulfed in flames. There was an explosion caused by someone accidentally putting gasoline instead of kerosene in the can. His 13 year old brother who accompanied him that day, died in the fire.

They dragged the unconscious little boy out of the flaming building more dead than alive. He had major burns over the lower half of his body and was taken to a nearby county hospital.

From his bed the dreadfully burned, semi-conscious little boy faintly heard the doctor talking to his mother. The doctor told his mother that her son would surely die – which was for the best, really – for the terrible fire had devastated the lower half of his body.

But the brave boy didn't want to die. He made up his mind that he would survive. Somehow, to the amazement of the physician, he did survive. When the mortal danger was past, he again heard the doctor and his mother speaking quietly. The mother was told that since the fire had destroyed so much flesh in the lower part of his body, it would almost be better if he had died, since he was doomed to be a lifetime cripple with no use at all of his lower limbs. The doctors recommended amputating his legs but he was so distressed his parents would not allow it.

Once more the brave boy made up his mind. He would not be a cripple. He would walk. But unfortunately from the waist down, he had no motor ability. His thin legs just dangled there, all but lifeless.

Ultimately he was released from the hospital. Every day his mother would massage his little legs, but there was no feeling, no control, nothing. Yet his determination that he would walk was as strong as ever.

When he wasn't in bed, he was confined to a wheelchair. One sunny day his mother wheeled him out into the yard to get some fresh air. This day, instead of sitting there, he threw himself from the chair. He pulled himself across the grass, dragging his legs behind him.

He worked his way to the white picket fence bordering their lot. With great effort, he raised himself up on the fence. Then, stake by stake, he began dragging himself along the fence, resolved that he would walk. He started to do this every day until he wore a smooth path all around the yard beside the fence. There was nothing he wanted more than to develop life in those legs.

Ultimately through his daily massages, his iron persistence and his resolute determination, he did develop the ability to stand up, then to walk haltingly, then to walk by himself – and then – to run.

He began to walk to school, then to run to school, to run for the sheer joy of running. Later in college he made the track team.

Still later in Madison Square Garden this young man who was not expected to survive, who would surely never walk, who could never hope to run – this determined young man, Dr. Glenn Cunningham, ran the world's fastest mile!

FIRM FAITH

He had a positive attitude as well as a strong religious faith. His favorite verse was Isaiah 40:31: "But those who wait on the Lord shall renew their strength; they shall mount up with wings like eagles, they shall run and not be weary, they shall walk and not faint."

BREAKING THE WORLD RECORD

On June 16, 1934, Glenn Cunningham ran the mile in 4:06.8 minutes, breaking the world's record. His effort portrays that whatever you want to create in your life is yours for the making. As long as you desire it enough and allow your will to guide you, you can have and be whatever your heart desires. The only one that can put limits on our personal will is ourselves. Develop and encourage your will to create and all the forces of nature within and without will help you bring your desire to pass.

It is simply a question of practice. In Bengal it is said, sarire nam mahasaya jasa babe tayse: "By practice you can train your body to tolerate almost anything." For example, in the morning, when we go for our walk, we see so many people running. I cannot run. But if I practice for some days, I will also be able to run. If you practice enough, you'll be successful at anything.

~ Srila Prabhupada (Acquiring a spiritual body takes practice)

LIFE SUMMARY

8 years old, was horribly burned in a schoolhouse fire. Doctors predicted he would never walk again.

22 months later, took his first steps and through sheer determination, learned to run despite the pain.

In high school, set records for the mile and later attended Kansas University.

While at Kansas, refused all scholarship money, preferring to pay his own way.

By sophomore year, ran the 1,500 meter race at the 1932 Olympics, but finished fourth due to a severe cold.

By senior year, set a world record for the mile of 4:06.8 and held seven of the top 13 fastest recorded times for the mile.

In 1936, voted "Most Popular Athlete" by his fellow athletes.

He went on to earn a master's degree from University of Iowa and later a doctorate from New York University.

He received the James E. Sullivan Award as the top amateur athlete in the United States in 1933.

While in New York, won 21 of 31 races at Madison Square Gardens and set an indoor mile record there in 1938. His fastest mile time was 4:04.4 at a Dartmouth track meet in 1938.

When the 1940 Olympics were cancelled, he retired from his running career and taught at Cornell College in Iowa.

During World War II, he served two years in the Navy.

Spent the remainder of his life running the Glenn Cunningham Youth Ranch for troubled kids in Kansas, USA. It is estimated that

he and his wife raised around 9,000 kids on their ranch in the years until his death in 1988.

To verify this amazing true story, see the Glenn Cunningham article on the Kansas Sports Hall of Fame's website at http://www.kshof.org/inductees/cunningham.html.

Cunningham was inducted into the National Track and Field Hall of Fame in 1974.

Source

Burt Dubin, Speaking Success System.

Stephen. The power of determination, August 29, 2012, Awakening, True Stories

Glenn Cunningham, Kansas Sports Hall of Fame,

http://www.kshof.org/inductees/cunningham.html

"Cool Things - Olympic Village Letter". Cool Things. Kansas Historical Society.

"City of Elkhart Ks".

American Miler, Paul J. Kiell, M.D., p. 105

Glenn Cunningham MyBestYears.com Interview Spotlight

IF YOU'RE GOING THROUGH HELL

KEEP GOING

One day a young lady was driving along with her father. They came upon a storm and the young lady asked her father, "What should I do?"

Father, a meteorologist, said, "Keep driving." Cars began to pull over to the side, the storm was getting worse.

"What should I do?" The young lady asked?

"Keep driving," her father replied.

On up a few feet, she noticed that eighteen wheelers were also pulling over. She told her father, "I must pull over, I can barely see ahead. It is terrible and everyone is pulling over!"

Her father told her, "Don't give up, just keep driving!"

Now the storm was terrible, but she never stopped driving and soon she could see a little more clearly. After a couple of miles she was again on dry land and the sun came out.

Her father said, "Now you can pull over and get out."

Young Lady said, "But why now?"

Father said, "When you get out, look back at all the people that gave up and are still in the storm, because you never gave up your storm is now over."

Next day's newspapers covered the stories of drivers trapped in the storm and their vehicles thrown asunder.

This is a testimony for anyone who is going through "hard times." Just because everyone else, even the strongest, gives up, you don't have to ... if you keep going, soon your storm will be over and the Sun will shine upon your face again.

Reference

Larry O'Sullivan, How Is My Driving?: Motivational Tips For Success In Business And Life, AuthorHouse.

Harriet Sime, Just When The Zeal Is Slipping Away, April 2001.

samasrita ye pada-pallava-plavam
mahat-padam punya-yaso murareh
bhavambudhir vatsa-padam param padam
padam padam yad vipadam na tesam
"For one who has accepted the boat of the lotus feet of the Lord, who is the shelter of the cosmic manifestation and is famous as Mukunda, or the giver of mukti, the ocean of the material world is like the water contained in a calf's footprint. param padam, or the place where there are no material miseries, or Vaikuntha, is his goal, not the place where there is danger in every step of life."
~ Srimad Bhagavatam (10.14.58)

YOUR BELIEFS

CREATE YOUR REALITY

A group of frogs were hopping contentedly through the woods, going about their froggy business, when two of them fell into a deep pit. All of the other frogs gathered around the pit to see what could be done to help their companions. When they saw how deep the pit was, the rest of the dismayed group agreed that it was hopeless and told the two frogs in the pit that they should prepare themselves for their fate, because they were as good as dead.

Unwilling to accept this terrible fate, the two frogs began to jump with all of their might.

Some of the frogs shouted into the pit that it was hopeless and that the two frogs would not be in that situation if they had been more careful, more obedient to the froggy rules, and more responsible. The other frogs continued sorrowfully shouting that they should save their energy and give up, since they were already as good as dead.

The two frogs continued jumping as hard as they could and after several hours of desperate effort were quite weary.

> *Your beliefs become your thoughts*
> *Your thoughts become your words*
> *Your words become your actions*
> *Your actions become your habits*
> *Your habits become your values*
> *Your values become your destiny*

Finally, one of the frogs took heed to the calls of his fellows. Spent and disheartened, he quietly resolved himself to his fate, lay down at the bottom of the pit and died as the others looked on in helpless grief. The other frog continued to jump with every ounce of energy he had, although his body was wracked with pain and he was completely exhausted.

His companions began a new, yelling for him to accept his fate, stop the pain and just die. The weary frog jumped harder and harder and -

sri-prahlada uvaca
tat sadhu manye 'sura-varya dehinam
sada samudvigna-dhiyam asad-grahat
hitvatma-patam grham andha-kupam
vanam gato yad dharim asrayeta

Prahlada Maharaja replied: O best of the asuras, King of the demons, as far as I have learned from my spiritual master, any person who has accepted a temporary body and temporary household life is certainly embarrassed by anxiety because of having fallen in a dark well where there is no water but only suffering. One should give up this position and go to the forest [vana]. More clearly, one should go to Vrndavana, where only Krsna consciousness is prevalent, and should thus take shelter of the Supreme Personality of Godhead.

~ Srimad Bhagavatam 7.5.5

wonder of wonders! Finally leapt so high that he sprang from the pit. Amazed, the other frogs celebrated his miraculous freedom and then gathering around him asked, "Why did you continue jumping when we told you it was impossible?" Reading their lips, the astonished frog explained to them that he was deaf and that when he saw their gestures and shouting, he thought they were cheering him on.

What he had perceived as encouragement inspired him to try harder and to succeed against all odds.

Reference

Justin Lewis, Firefighter Self Rescue: The Evolution of Service, iUniverse.

Katherine Rushton, Hope Against Hope, June 1996.

The power of words:

This simple Frog story contains a powerful lesson. Encouraging or positive words can lift someone up and help him or her make it through the day. Destructive or negative words can cause deep wounds; they may be the weapons that destroy someone's desire to continue trying - or even their life.

Affliction caused by the tongue is worse than that caused by the strike of the blade of a sword. Be careful of what you say. Speak life to those who cross your path.

Words can be weapons. Words can wound, humiliate and inflict pain far greater than physical violence. Words can be used to inflame passions, to arouse anger, to declare war and to destroy. But just as potent as they are as weapons, words can also heal wounds and make peace. They can be soothing to those in grief, they can offer hope to those in despair. Indeed, well-chosen words have a power and a beauty that can project well beyond one lifetime. Think of the great works of literature that still enrich our lives today, centuries after they were written.

Keep Your Head Cool And Your Heart Warm

To Get Out of a "No Way Out" Situation

Many years ago in a small Indian village, a farmer had the misfortune of owing a large sum of money to a village moneylender. The moneylender, who was old and ugly, fancied the farmer's beautiful daughter. So he proposed a bargain. He said he would forgo the farmer's debt if he could marry his daughter.

Both the farmer and his daughter were horrified by the proposal. So the cunning money-lender suggested that they let providence decide the matter. He told them that he would put a black pebble and a white pebble into an empty money bag. Then the girl would have to pick one pebble from the bag.

If she picked the black pebble, she would become his wife and her father's debt would be forgiven. If she picked the white pebble she need not marry him and her father's debt would still be forgiven. If she refused to pick a pebble, her father would be thrown into jail.

News of the moneylender's proposal quickly spread and a crowd gathered. They were standing on a pebble strewn path in the farmer's field. As they talked, the moneylender bent over to pick up two pebbles. As he picked them up, the sharp-eyed girl noticed that he had picked up two black pebbles and put them into the bag. He then asked the girl to pick a pebble from the bag.

Now, imagine that you were standing in the field. What would you have done if you were the girl? If you had to advise her, what would you have told her?

Take a moment to ponder this. What would you recommend that the girl do?

The girl put her hand into the moneybag and drew out a pebble. Without looking at it, she fumbled and let it fall onto the pebble-strewn path where it immediately became lost among all the other pebbles.

"Oh, how clumsy of me!" she said. "But never mind, if you look into the bag for the one that is left, you will be able to tell which pebble I picked."

The moneylender dared not admit his dishonesty in front of the assembled crowd. The girl changed what seemed an impossible situation into an extremely advantageous one.

> *sarvasya caham hrdi sannivisto*
> *mattah smrtir jnanam apohanam ca*
>
> *I am seated in everyone's heart, and from Me come remembrance, knowledge and forgetfulness. By all the Vedas, I am to be known. Indeed, I am the compiler of Vedanta, and I am the knower of the Vedas.*
> ~ *Bhagavad-gita 15.15*

Reference

Dan Miller, No More Mondays: Fire Yourself -- and Other Revolutionary Ways to Discover Efficiency, Crown Publishing Group

Jack White, Malady of Art: FEAR

David Boud, Ruth Cohen, Jane Sampson, Peer Learning in Higher Education: Learning from & with Each Other, Psychology Press.

FEED YOUR FAITH

AND YOUR FEARS WILL STARVE TO DEATH

FAITH IS THE FOUNDATION ON WHICH ALL THE OTHER VIRTUES ARE BUILT

When we build a house, we take so much care to have a strong foundation so that it can stand the test of weather and time or that we could build more above it in course of time.

Do we take care to build our lives too on a strong faith foundation to courageously face the storms and challenges in life?

To stress the need to have strong faith, Jesus told of a parable of a wise man and foolish man who ventured to build a house. The wise man built his house upon the rock. The foolish man built his house upon the sand. The rains came down, the floods rose and gales and storms beat against the houses. The foolish man's house crashed to the ground while the wise man's house stood firm.

Most of us have experiences of facing storms. There could be financial storms, relationship storms, emotional storms, physical storms (health problems). People who build there lives on a strong faith foundation are those who will face the storm calmly and survive.

People try to give their children the best of education, food, clothing, entertainment. But the most beautiful gift they can give their children is the gift of strong faith in God. Such children will be able to stand the challenges and storms of life courageously even when the parents are not around anymore.

A story is told of a shipwreck where everyone was swimming to safety. One sailor was struggling to make it to the shore when he

> There are three types of faith, corresponding to and evolving from the three modes of material nature. Acts performed by those whose faith is in passion and ignorance yield only impermanent, material results, whereas acts performed in goodness, in accord with scriptural injunctions, purify the heart and lead to pure faith in Lord Krsna and devotion to Him.
>
> sattvanurupa sarvasya
> sraddha bhavati bharata
> sraddha-mayo 'yam puruso
> yo yac-chraddhah sa eva sah
>
> O son of Bharata, according to one's existence under the various modes of nature, one evolves a particular kind of faith. The living being is said to be of a particular faith according to the modes he has acquired.
>
> ~ Bhagavad-gita 17: The Divisions of Faith

suddenly saw a small rock protruding above the tide. He gripped to it tightly till the storm subsided. When he reached the shore, people asked him "Did you not shake with fear when you held that small rock?" He quipped "Yes, I shook with fear, but the Rock did not shake and that's why I am alive right now."

Let us give ourselves and our children that rock to hold on to. When a pious man was on his deathbed he called all his children

Without faith we cannot make any progress. In any field of activity we must have faith. For example, I cited the other day, just like we go to a barber shop, and we spread our neck, and the barber has got a sharp razor in his hand. If he likes, he can at once cut my throat. He has got the weapon ready. But because I have got faith he'll not do it -- he'll simply shave my beard or mustaches... So this faith is required in every activity. Without faith we cannot step forward even in our daily life. So if we have to have so much faith in ordinary dealings, don't you think that we must have very good faith when we are making progress in spiritual line?

Suppose I am going to California from here, from New York. I have to purchase an air ticket. Now, I must have faith that "This airline will take me to there." There may be some accident, but on faith I accept it, "Yes, it will take me there." Who knows that this airplane will take me to California? It may go down to hell. Or even if I take a bus or train, there may be some accident. There is possibility. But on faith we accept. So if we want to make progress, material or spiritual, we must have faith.

And where to keep our faith? In the authority. I am not going to book my ticket with an unauthorized company. Similarly, here we must have faith in Krsna. If you have got this faith in Krsna or Jesus Christ or whatever you may have.... Without faith, you cannot make progress. That is called faithful. And those who have no faith, they are called faithless. So here it is clearly stated, sraddhavan labhate jnanam: "Those who are faithful, they can make progress in this knowledge of spiritual advancement."

And faith, how we become faithful? Now, samyata indriya. You have to control the senses. Our material existence is here because we want to gratify senses. That is the whole disease. Just like if you are taking treatment of a physician and you have faith in his treatment. But the physician says, "Don't do this," and if you do this, then what kind of faith you have got?

~ Srila Prabhupada (Lecture, Bhagavad-gita 4.37-40 -- New York, August 21, 1966)

around him and said, "My children, if I leave all my wealth and property for you but do not leave you with a strong faith in God, you will be poor, very poor. But If I do not leave you any wealth or property but leave you with a strong faith in God, you will be rich, very rich indeed."

Reference:

Thomas Boston, Human Nature in Its Fourfold State,

Matthew 7:24-27

Sananda, Judas Iscarioth, And They Called His Name Immanuel: I Am Sananda, Phoenix Source Distributors, Inc.

Elbert Hubbard, Elbert Hubbard's Scrap Book: Containing the Inspired and Inspiring Selections, Pelican Publishing Company.

Stuart Nettleton, The Alchemy Key: The Mystical Provenance of the Philosophers Stone, Taliesin Investments, 1997

YOU CAN START A BUSINESS

EVEN WITH A DEAD MOUSE

WHERE THERE'S WILL, THERE'S A WAY

(Following story about a Calcutta businessman was narrated by Srila Prabhupada in a Class in Vrindavan in August of 1974)

A mercantile man will find out some business. There is a practical story. Long ago in Calcutta, one Mr. Nandi went to some friend with a request, "If you can give me a little capital, I can start some business." The friend replied, "You are a vaisya, a mercantile man." "Yes." "So, why are you asking money from me? Money's lying on the street. You can go and pick." Mr. Nandi said, "I don't see any."

"You don't see? Look, what is that?"

"That, that is a dead mouse."

"That is your capital."

So in those days plague was going on in Calcutta. There was a municipal declaration that if any one brought a dead mouse to the municipal office, he'll be paid two annas. So he took the dead mouse to the municipal office and collected his two annas.

With those two annas, he purchased some rotten betel nuts and after washing thoroughly, sold them for four annas. In this way, trading again and again he multiplied his capital and became a rich man. One of their family members was our Godbrother.

Even today in this Nandi family, four or five hundred men eat daily. It is a big, aristocratic family.

And their family's rule is, as soon as a son or daughter is born, five thousand rupees are deposited in the bank, and at the time of their marriage, that five thousand rupees with interest, they can take it. They have no further claim on the family's capital. And everyone who lives in the family, he is provided with food and shelter. It's a big family but the founder of this family, Mr Nandi started his business with a dead mouse.

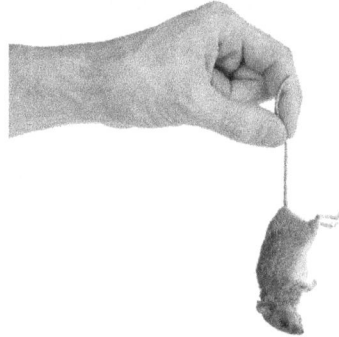

That is actually a fact, that if one wants to live independently, without become a slave of somebody, he can do so by finding some means of livelihood. In Calcutta I have seen. Even poor class vaisyas, in the morning they'll take some dal, a bag of dal (pulses), and go door to door. Dal is required everywhere. So in the morning he makes dal business, and in the evening he takes a canister of kerosene oil. In the evening everyone requires that. Still you'll find in India, not many are seeking employment. Selling something, whatever they have got, even some groundnuts or peanuts. Something they're doing. After all, Krsna is giving maintenance to everyone. It is a mistake to think that "This man is giving me maintenance." No. *Sastra* says, *eko yo bahunam vidadhati kaman.* It is confidence in Krsna, that "Krsna has given me life, Krsna has sent me here. So He'll give me my maintenance. So according to my capacity, let me do something, and through that source, Krsna's maintenance will come."

Reference
Srila Prabhupada, Lecture, Srimad-Bhagavatam 1.5.22 -- Vrndavana, August 3, 1974

RAGS TO RICHES

INCREDIBLE STORIES OF HARD WORK PAYING OFF

This is an account of some rich and famous people who never gave up in life. In spite of the setbacks, they chose to fight on.

"I slept on benches and everyday borrowed 20 Rs. from friend to travel to film city" - Sharukh khan (Indian film star)

"I failed in 8th standard"
-Sachin Tendulkar (Indian cricket legend)

"During my secondary school, I was dropped from school basketball team" -Michael Jordan (American basketball legend)

"I was rejected for the job in All India Radio because of my heavy voice" - Amitabh Bacchan (Indian film star)

"I used to work in a petrol pump" - Dhirubhai Ambani (Indian billionaire)

"I didn't even complete my university education" - Bill Gates (Microsoft Founder)

"I was a dyslexic kid" - Tom Cruise (Hollywood star)

"I was raped at the age of 9 " - Oprah Winfrey (American media magnate)

"I used to serve tea at a shop to support my football training"
- Lionel Messi (Argentine footballer)

"I didn't have a dorm room, so I slept on the floor in friends' rooms. I returned coke bottles for the 5¢ deposits to buy food with. And I would walk the 7 miles across town every Sunday night to get one good meal a week at the Hare Krishna temple. -Steve Jobs (Apple CEO)

"My teachers used to call me a failure" - Tony Blair (British Prime Minister)

"I was in prison for 27 years" - Late President Nelson Mandela

"At the age of 30, I was a bus conductor" - Rajnikant (South Indian film legend)

"As a kid, I was selling tea on the railway station." - Narendra Modi (Indian Prime Minister)

Life is not about what you couldn't do so far, it's about what you can still do.

Those who are convinced for making a sure progress of life, they're called niscayatmika buddhih. That is determination. Drdha-vrata, drdha-vrata. These are Sanskrit words: "firmly convinced, steady." They have got only one business, one business. Vyavasayatmika buddhir ekeha...bahu-sakha hy anantas ca... Those who are not steady, they have got many business, many business. Why many? If that one is the source of everything, take that one.

The example is that just like the root of the tree is the source of distribution of energy. Then pour water in the root, not in the leaves, not in the branches. So people are enamored by the branches and leaves and flowers. They are inventing so many societies, humanitarian societies, altruistic societies, nonviolent societies, United Nation, this, that, all nonsense. Simply concentrate on Krsna consciousness. Everything will be right. That they do not know. This is intelligence, how to act. Just work on one switch, and everything will be right. That they do not know.

~ Srila Prabhupada (Lecture, Srimad-Bhagavatam 1.5.13 -- New Vrindaban, June 16, 1969)

In Order To Attain The Impossible

One Must Attempt The Absurd

It Always Seems Impossible Until It's Done

In 1867, a creative engineer named John Roebling was inspired by an idea to build a spectacular bridge connecting New York with the Long Island. However bridge building experts throughout the world thought that this was an impossible feat and told John Roebling to forget the idea. It just could not be done. It was not practical. It had never been done before.

John Roebling could not ignore the vision he had in his mind of this bridge. He thought about it all the time and he knew deep in his heart that it could be done. He just had to share the dream with someone else.

THE BROOKLYN ANCHORAGE.

After much discussion and persuasion he managed to convince his son Washington Roebling, an upcoming engineer, that the bridge in fact could be built.

Working together for the first time, the father and son developed concepts of how it could be accomplished and how the obstacles could be overcome. With great excitement and inspiration, and the headiness of a wild challenge before them, they hired their crew and began to build their dream bridge.

The project started well, but when it was only a few months underway a tragic accident on the site took the life of John Roebling. Washington Roebling was injured and left with a certain amount of brain damage, which resulted in him not being able to walk or talk or even move.

"We told them so. Crazy men and their crazy dreams. It's foolish to chase wild visions."

Everyone had a negative comment to make and felt that the project should be scrapped since the Roeblings were the only ones who knew how the bridge could be built. In spite of his handicap Washington Roebling was never discouraged and still had a burning desire to complete the bridge and his mind was still as sharp as ever.

Washington Roebling tried to inspire and pass on his enthusiasm to some of his friends, but they were too daunted by the task. As

Determination means that one has to continue with patience and perseverance. I'm not getting the desired result. "Oh what is this, I give up." No. Determination. It is a fact. Because Krsna is saying this it must happen. There is nice example. That a girl is married to a husband. She's hankering after a child. So if she thinks that "Now I am married, I must have immediately a child." Is it possible? Just have patience. You just become faithful wife, serve your husband, and let your love grow up and because you are husband and wife, it is sure you'll have children. But don't be impatient. Similarly, when you are in Krsna consciousness, your perfection is guaranteed. But you'll have to have patience, determination. That "I must execute. I should not be impatient." That impatience is due to loss of determination.

~ Srila Prabhupada (Lecture, Bhagavad-gita 6.16-24 -- Los Angeles, February 17, 1969)

he lay on his bed in his hospital room, with the sunlight streaming through the windows, a gentle breeze blew the flimsy white curtains apart and he was able to see the sky and the tops of the trees outside for just a moment.

It seemed that there was a message for him not to give up. Suddenly

John A. Roebling   Washington Roebling   Emily Warren Roebling

an idea hit him. All he could do was move one finger and he decided to make the best use of it. By moving this, he slowly developed a code of communication with his wife Emily.

Washington Roebling touched his wife's arm with that finger, conveying to her that he wanted her to call the engineers again. Then he used the same method of tapping her arm to tell the engineers what to do. It seemed foolish but the project was under way again.

For 13 years Washington Roebling tapped out his instructions with his finger on his wife's arm, until the bridge was finally completed in 1883. Today the spectacular Brooklyn Bridge stands in all its glory as a tribute to the triumph of one man's indomitable spirit and his determination not to be defeated by circumstances. It is also a tribute to the engineers and their team work, and to their faith in a man who was considered mad by half the world. It stands too as a tangible monument to the love and devotion of his wife who for 13 long years patiently decoded the messages of her husband Washington Roebling and told the engineers what to do.

Perhaps this is one of the best examples of a never-say-die attitude that overcomes a terrible physical handicap and achieves an impossible goal.

Often when we face obstacles in our day-to-day life, our hurdles seem very small in comparison to what many others have to face. The Brooklyn Bridge shows us that dreams that seem impossible can be realized with determination and persistence, no matter what the odds are.

"Never tell a young person that anything cannot be done. God may have been waiting centuries for someone ignorant enough of the impossible to do that very thing." - G. M. Trevelyan

Reference

Richard G. Weingardt, Engineering Legends: Great American Civil Engineers, American Society of Civil Engineers

Washington Roebling, Washington Roebling's Father: A Memoir of John A. Roebling, ASCE Press

Charles Landry, The Art of City Making, Routledge Inc.

David E. Nye, American Technological Sublime, MIT Press

SOMETIMES YOU DON'T REALIZE YOUR OWN STRENGTH

UNTIL YOU COME FACE TO FACE WITH YOUR GREATEST WEAKNESS

A jobless man applied for the position of 'office boy' at a very big firm.

The HR manager interviewed him, then a test: clean the floor. "You are hired" he said, give me your email address, and I will send you the application to fill, as well as when you will start. The man replied "I don't have a computer, neither an email".

I am sorry, said the HR manager, if you don't have an email that means you do not exist. And who doesn't exist, cannot have the job. The man left with no hope at all. He didn't know what to do, with only $10 in his pocket.

He then decided to go to the supermarket and buy a 10 KG Tomato crate. He then sold the Tomatoes in a door to door round. In less than two hours, he succeeded to double his capital. He repeated the operation 3 times, and returned home with $60 US. The man realized that he can survive by this way, and started to go everyday earlier, and return late. Thus, his money doubles or triples every day.

Shortly later, he bought a cart, then a truck, and then he had his own fleet of delivery vehicles.

5 years later, the man is one of the biggest food retailers in the US. He started to plan his family's future, and decided to have a life insurance.

He called an insurance broker, and chose a protection plan. When the conversation was concluded, the broker asked him his email. The man replied: 'I don't have an email'. The broker replied curiously, you don't have an email, and yet have succeeded to build an empire. Do you imagine what you could have been if you had an email?

The man thought for a while, and replied: an office boy!

Reference

Alan Axelrod, The Complete Idiot's Guide to American History, Alpha Books

Chris Gardner, Mim E. Rivas, Start Where You Are: Life Lessons in Getting from Where You Are to Where You Want To Be, Harper Collins.

David Teten, Scott Allen, The Virtual Handshake: Opening Doors and Closing Deals Online, AMACOM Div American Mgmt Assn.

tasyaiva hetoh prayateta kovido
na labhyate yad bhramatam upary adhah
tal labhyate duhkhavad anyatah sukham
kalena sarvatra gabhira-ramhasa

Persons who are actually intelligent and philosophically inclined should endeavor only for that purposeful end which is not obtainable even by wandering from the topmost planet [Brahmaloka] down to the lowest planet [Patala]. As far as happiness derived from sense enjoyment is concerned, it can be obtained automatically in course of time, just as in course of time we obtain miseries even though we do not desire them.

~ *Srimad Bhagavatam 1.5.18*

YOUR BIGGEST WEAKNESS

CAN BECOME YOUR BIGGEST STRENGTH

YOU NEVER KNOW HOW STRONG YOU ARE UNTIL BEING STRONG IS THE ONLY CHOICE YOU HAVE

This is a story of a 10-year-old boy who decided to study Judo despite the fact that he had lost his left arm in a devastating car accident.

The boy began lessons with an old Japanese Judo master. The boy was doing well, so he couldn't understand why, after three months of training the master had taught him only one move.

"Sensei," the boy finally said, "Shouldn't I be learning more moves?"

"This is the only move you know, but this is the only move you'll ever need to know," the Sensei replied. (Sensei in martial arts refers to a teacher.)

Not quite understanding, but believing in his teacher, the boy kept training.

Several months later, the sensei took the boy to his first tournament. Surprising himself, the boy easily won his first two matches. The third match proved to be more difficult, but after some time, his opponent became impatient and charged; the boy deftly used his one move to win the match.

Still amazed by his success, the boy was now in the finals.

This time, his opponent was bigger, stronger, and more experienced. For a while, the boy appeared to be overmatched. Concerned that the boy might get hurt, the referee called a time-out. He was about to stop the match when the Sensei intervened.

"No," the Sensei insisted, "Let him continue."

Soon after the match resumed, his opponent made a critical mistake: He dropped his guard. Instantly, the boy used his move to pin him. The boy had won the match and the tournament. He was the champion.

On the way home, the boy and Sensei reviewed every move in each and every match. Then the boy summoned the courage to ask what was really on his mind.

"Sensei, how did I win the tournament with only one move?"

"You won for two reasons," the Sensei answered. "First, you've almost mastered one of the most difficult throws in all of Judo. And second, the only known defense for that move is for your opponent to grab your left arm."

We should always be enthusiastic to try for shooting the rhinoceros. That way, if we fail, everybody will say, "Never mind, nobody can shoot a rhinoceros anyway," and if we succeed, then everyone will say, "Just see, what a wonderful thing they have done."
~ Srila Prabhupada (Letter to Balavanta Dasa, 1971)

The moral of this story: The boy's biggest weakness had become his biggest strength.

Reference

Meir Liraz, The 100 Top Inspirational Anecdotes and Stories: A collection of witty, Inspiring Stories, Liraz Publishing.

Robert E. Reed, Character Coins, Xulon Press

Lyndall Briggs, Gary Green, Soul Purpose: Self Development Stories, Quotes and Poems

sukha-duhkhe same krtva
labhalabhau jayajayau
tato yuddhaya yujyasva
naivam papam avapsyasi
Do thou fight for the sake of fighting without considering happiness or distress, loss or gain.
~ Bhagavad-gita 2.38

YOU CAN SUCCEED IN LIFE

EVEN IF YOU ARE AN UNDERACHIEVER CRACKPOT

Once upon a time there was a water-bearer in India who had two large pots, each hung on each end of a pole which he carried across his neck. One of the pots had a crack in it, and while the other pot was perfect and always delivered a full portion of water at the end of the long walk from the stream to the master's house, the cracked pot arrived only half full.

For a full two years this went on daily, with the bearer delivering only one and a half pot full of water in his master's house.

Of course, the perfect pot was proud of its accomplishments, perfect to the end for which it was made. But the poor cracked pot

> *Just like Dhruva Maharaja. He did not know how to achieve the favor of Supreme Personality of Godhead, but on account of his eagerness... He wanted to see God. Because he was a ksatriya... His mother said that "God only can help you, my dear son. If you want to become a king and sit on the throne of your father, then only God can help you. I cannot help you." So he was determined, "I must see God." Then he went to the forest but he did not know how to approach God. A boy of five years old only, he has got the determination. So Krsna saw that "This boy is very determined." Therefore He sent His representative, Narada: "Go and train him. He is very eager."*
>
> *~ Srila Prabhupada (Lecture, Srimad-Bhagavatam 6.1.16 -- Honolulu, May 16, 1976)*

was ashamed of its own imperfection, and miserable that it was able to accomplish only half of what it had been made to do.

After two years of what it perceived to be a bitter failure, it spoke to the water-bearer one day by the stream. "I am ashamed of myself, and I want to apologize to you." "Why?" asked the bearer.

"What are you ashamed of ?"

"I have been able, for these past two years, to deliver only half my load because this crack in my side causes water to leak out all the way back to your master's house. Because of my flaws, you have to do all of this work and you don't get full value from your efforts, " the pot said.

The water-bearer felt sorry for the old cracked pot and replied, "As we return to the master's house, I want you to notice the beautiful flowers along the path."

Indeed, as they went up the hill, the old cracked pot took notice of the sun warming the beautiful wild flowers on the side of the path, and this cheered it some.

But at the end of the trail, it still felt bad because it had leaked out half its load, and so again it apologized to the bearer for its failure.

The bearer said to the pot, "Did you notice that there were flowers only on your side of your path, but not on the other pot's side?

That's because I have always known about your flaw, and I took advantage of it. I planted flower seeds on your side of the path, and every day while we walk back from the stream, you've watered them. For two years I have been able to pick these beautiful flowers to decorate the Lord's temple. Without you being just the way you are, you could not have contributed to the world in this beautiful manner.

Each of us have our own unique flaws. But we can utilize these very cracks and flaws to make the world a better place. These cracks and flaws can make our lives so very interesting and rewarding, if dovetailed in the service of the world.

You've just have to accept yourself for what you are and look for the good in yourself.

Reference:

Robert Fulghum, It Was On Fire When I Lay Down On It, Random House Publishing Group

Judith Valente, Atchison Blue: A Search for Silence, a Spiritual Home, and a Living Faith

Abi Rowsell, A Gift of Happiness, MQ Publications Limited

THE BEST WAY TO MAKE YOUR DREAMS COME TRUE

IS TO WAKE UP

DREAMS ARE THE TOUCHSTONES OF YOUR CHARACTER

A young man named Monty Roberts owns a horse ranch in San Ysidro. A group of visitors came to see his beautiful ranch. He narrated his life story to them.

"I want to tell you something about my life. It all goes back to a story about a young man who was the son of an itinerant horse trainer who would go from stable to stable, race track to race track, farm to farm and ranch to ranch, training horses. As a result, the boy's high school career was continually interrupted. When he was a senior, he was asked to write a paper about what he wanted to be and do when he grew up."

"That night he wrote a seven-page paper describing his goal of someday owning a horse ranch. He wrote about his dream in great detail and he even drew a diagram of a 200-acre ranch, showing the location of all the buildings, the stables and the track. Then he drew a detailed floor plan for a 4,000-square-foot house that would sit on a 200-acre dream ranch."

"He put a great deal of his heart into the project and the next day he handed it in to his teacher. Two days later he received his paper back. On the front page was a large red F with a note that read, `See me after class.'"

"The boy with the dream went to see the teacher after class and asked, `Why did I receive an F?'"

"The teacher said, `This is an unrealistic dream for a young boy like you. You have no money. You come from an itinerant family. You have no resources. Owning a horse ranch requires a lot of money. You have to buy the land. You have to pay for the original breeding stock and later you'll have to pay large stud fees. There's no way you could ever do it.' Then the teacher added, `If you will rewrite this paper with a more realistic goal, I will reconsider your grade.'"

"The boy went home and thought about it long and hard. He asked his father what he should do. His father said, `Look, son, you have to make up your own mind on this. However, I think it is a very important decision for you.' Finally, after sitting with it for a week, the boy turned in the same paper, making no changes at all.

He stated, `You can keep the F and I'll keep my dream.'"

vyavasayatmika buddhir
ekeha kuru-nandana
bahu-sakha hy anantas ca
buddhayo 'vyavasayinam
Those who are on this path are resolute in purpose, and their aim is one. O beloved child of the Kurus, the intelligence of those who are irresolute is many-branched.
~ *Bhagavad-gita 2.41*

Monty then turned to the assembled group and said, "I tell you this story because you are sitting in my 4,000-square-foot house in the middle of my 200-acre horse ranch. I still have that school paper framed over the fireplace."

He added, "The best part of the story is that two summers ago that same schoolteacher brought 30 kids to camp out on my ranch for a week. When the teacher was leaving, the teacher said, 'Look, Monty, I can tell you this now. When I was your teacher, I was something of a dream stealer. During those years I stole a lot of kids' dreams. Fortunately you had enough gumption not to give up on yours.'"

"Don't let anyone steal your dreams. Follow your heart, no matter what."

Reference

T.C. Boyle, The Inner Circle, Penguin Books

Keep Your Dream by Stephen, October, 2008

The Shape of a Pocket, John Berger, Knopf Doubleday Publishing Group

John Berger, Selected Essays of John Berger, Knopf Doubleday Publishing Group

Don't Give Up, Ever

No Matter What

by Morty Lefkoe

How would you be living your life today if you hadn't been able to speak until you were almost 4 years old and your teachers said you "would never amount to much"? Please take a moment and answer this question right now. You will learn something very important.

It happened to Albert Einstein, who went on to become one of the most influential scientists of all time.

How would you be living your life today if your life was totally about basketball and you had been cut from your high school basketball team? Please take a moment and answer this question right now. You will learn something very important.

It happened to Michael Jordan, who went on to become one of the best basketball players ever.

How would you be living your life today if you had been fired from a newspaper for "lacking imagination and "having no original

Life is like a piano the white keys represent happiness and the black shows sadness. but as you go through life's journey, remember that the black keys also make music

ideas"? Please take a moment and answer this question right now. You will learn something very important.

It happened to Walt Disney, who went on to create a successful movie studio that developed many innovative cartoons and cartoon characters.

How would you be living your life today if at the age of 30 you had been fired from the company you had founded and devoted your entire adult life to? Please take a moment and answer this question right now. You will learn something very important.

It happened to Steve Jobs, who went on to revolutionize life as we knew it by leading one of the most imaginative and successful companies in history.

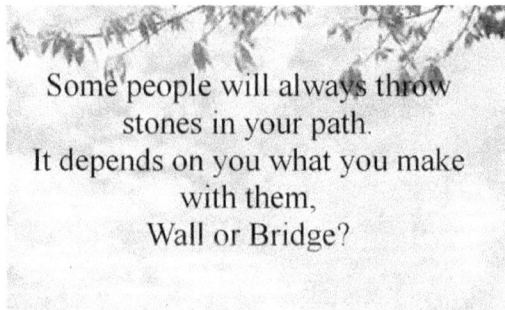

Some people will always throw stones in your path. It depends on you what you make with them, Wall or Bridge?

How would you be living your life today if you had been demoted from your job as a news anchor because you were "not fit for television"? Please take a moment and answer this question right now. You will learn something very important.

It happened to Oprah Winfrey, who went on to become the most successful daytime host ever and one of the most recognized and inspirational figures in the world due to her television show.

How would you be living your life today if you had a band that had been rejected by Decca Records who said "we don't like their sound, they have no future in show business"? Please take a moment and answer this question right now. You will learn something very important.

It happened to the Beatles, which went on to revolutionize music and become one of the most successful bands in musical history.

How would these situations have affected you?

How did you answer these questions? Unfortunately, far too many people would answer that the disappointment led to a sense of victimization and a decision (perhaps unconscious) to not put themselves in a position where they could be disappointed again. Many if not most people would have quit.

How incidents like these lead many to conclude: I'll never get what I want. I'm inadequate. Life is difficult. If I allow myself to really want things, I'll be disappointed and get hurt. I'm not good enough.

> The tiny seed knew that in order to grow, it needed to be dropped in dirt, covered in darkness, struggle to reach the light.
>
> —Sandra Kring

And when people form beliefs like these, they either quit trying or, at best, they approach their goals with only a half-hearted commitment.

There is no such thing as a "failure"

The reason for telling you these "failure" stories is to remind you that not getting what you want at one point in your life does not mean you will never succeed. Each of these people ultimately became major successes in their respective fields. Their early "failures" did not stop them because they held these events as learning opportunities, not failures.

If you had major disappointments early in your life and you've stopped doing all you could possibly do to get what you want today, here's what to do -- right now.

HERE'S WHAT TO DO

First, identify and eliminate any beliefs you formed in response to the events. The beliefs I listed above are typical beliefs one might form in response to a major disappointment.

Second, recognize that no matter what happened, it does not mean you "failed." Failure is meaning you add to an event. In the case of

the six stories I told, none of the people ultimately experienced their setback as a failure. They held the "disappointment" as something they could learn from to make them successful in the future.

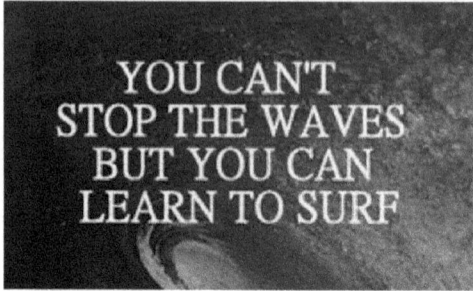

YOU CAN'T
STOP THE WAVES
BUT YOU CAN
LEARN TO SURF

Third, if you give negative meaning to events in your present life, notice you are doing that and make a clear distinction between what is actually happening (for example, things aren't turning out the way you would like them to) and the meaning you are giving the event (for example, you'll never succeed or you don't have the ability to ever succeed). What you make a clear distinction between the event and the meaning, the meaning will dissolve and

---

By practicing celibacy, one cultivates determination. One modern example of such determination is that of Mahatma Gandhi, who was determined to resist the powerful British empire by means of nonviolence. At this time, India was dependent on the British, and the people had no weapons. The Britishers, being more powerful, easily cut down whatever violent revolutions the people attempted. Therefore Gandhi resorted to nonviolence, noncooperation. "I shall not fight with the Britishers," he declared, "and even if they react with violence, I shall remain nonviolent. In this way the world will sympathize with us." Such a policy required a great amount of determination, and Gandhi's determination was very strong because he was a brahmacari. Although he had children and a wife, he renounced sex at the age of thirty-six. It was this sexual renunciation that enabled him to be so determined that he was able to lead his country and drive the British from India.

Thus, refraining from sex enables one to be very determined and powerful. It is not necessary to do anything else. This is a secret people are not aware of. If you want to do something with determination, you have to refrain from sex.

~ Srila Prabhupada (Path of Perfection 4: Moderation in Yoga)

all you will be left with is a meaningless event that is not capable of producing a negative feeling.

Fourth, stop allowing your beliefs and daily meanings to sabotage your life. It is possible for you to rid yourself of your self-imposed limitations (your beliefs and meanings) and to create unimagined new possibilities for your life. Start today.

Source
Morty Lefkoe
copyright ©2013 Morty Lefkoe

When The Pirates Attack

A navy captain is alerted by his First Mate that there is a pirate ship coming towards his position. He asks a sailor to get him his red shirt.

The captain was asked, "Why do you need a red shirt?"

The Captain replies, "So that when I bleed, you guys don't notice and aren't discouraged." They fight off the pirates eventually.

The very next day, the Captain is alerted that 50 pirate ships are coming towards their boat. He yells, "Get me my brown pants!"

SLOWLY

BUT SURELY

THE IMPORTANCE OF QUALITY OVER QUANTITY

There was the story about the expert craftsmanship of a plasterer who worked on the construction of the Taj Mahal. One of the top directors of the construction was inspecting the building in progress and noticed for three days in a row a certain plasterer who was sitting in the same place mixing plaster. On the third day the inspector became angry and said, "Why are you still simply sitting and mixing this plaster? You are so lazy!" The man who was mixing the plaster also became very angry, and he threw a handful

of his plaster at the inspector. The plaster missed the inspector but landed on a wall. The plaster was so well mixed, however, so solid and hard, that no one could get it off the wall, and it is still there today.

Srila Prabhupada told this story to stress the importance of good craftsmanship and of doing everything nicely in Krsna's service.

Reference

Srila Prabhupada Nectar 1-40: More Short Stories, Satsvarupa dasa Goswami

mukta-sango 'naham-vadi
dhrty-utsaha-samanvitah
siddhy-asiddhyor nirvikarah
karta sattvika ucyate
One who performs his duty without association with the modes of material nature, without false ego, with great determination and enthusiasm, and without wavering in success or failure is said to be a worker in the mode of goodness.

ragi karma-phala-prepsur
lubdho himsatmako 'sucih
harsa-sokanvitah karta
rajasah parikirtitah
The worker who is attached to work and the fruits of work, desiring to enjoy those fruits, and who is greedy, always envious, impure, and moved by joy and sorrow, is said to be in the mode of passion.

ayuktah prakrtah stabhah
satho naiskrtiko 'lasah
visadi dirgha-sutri ca
karta tamasa ucyate
The worker who is always engaged in work against the injunctions of the scripture, who is materialistic, obstinate, cheating and expert in insulting others, and who is lazy, always morose and procrastinating is said to be a worker in the mode of ignorance.

~ Bhagavad-gita 18.26 - 28

WORRY

IT'S A MISUSE OF IMAGINATION

IF THINGS GO WRONG, DON'T GO WITH THEM

D eath was walking toward a city one morning and a man asked, "What are you going to do?"

"I'm going to take 100 people," Death replied.

"That's horrible!" the man said.

"That's the way it is," Death said. "That's what I do."

The man hurried to warn everyone he could about Death's plan.

As evening fell, he met Death again. "You told me you were going to take 100 people," the man said. "Why did 1,000 die?"

"I kept my word," Death responded. "I only took 100 people. Worry took the others."

This interesting tale portrays so well what the US National Mental Health Committee reported a few years ago - half of all the people in America's hospital beds are constant worriers. Mental distress can lead to migraine headaches, arthritis, heart trouble, cystitis, colitis, backaches, ulcers, depression, digestive disorders and yes, even death. The mental fatigue

WHAT IF...?

98

of nights without sleep and days without peace, then we get a glimpse of the havoc worry plays in destroying the quality and quantity of life.

Worry is, and always will be, a fatal disease of the heart, for its beginning signals the end of faith.

Release the regrets of yesterday, refuse the fears of tomorrow and receive instead, the peace of today.

Blessed is the person who is too busy to worry in the daytime and too sleepy to worry at night.

Reference

Donald Archey, Pastor, How Did You Get AIDS? Tate Publishing

Andres Lara, Inspire The Sleeping Giant Within!: Brief, Simple Yet Profound Life-Altering Messages & Stories, Morris Pub., 2003

David G. Myers, Pursuit of Happiness, HarperCollins, June 1993

Chaitanya Mahaprabhu says that the actual identity of every living creature is that he is the eternal servant of God. And after one has realized that, then all one's cares and anxieties in this world are over because one knows, "I am a servant of God. God will give me protection. Why should I worry about anything?" It is just like a child. A child knows that his mother and father will take care of him. He is free. If he should go to touch fire, his mother will take care of him: "Oh, my dear child, don't touch." The mother is always looking after him. So why don't you put your trust in God? Actually, you are under the protection of God.

People go to church and say, "God, give us our daily bread." Actually, if He did not give it to us, we would not be able to live. That is a fact. The Vedas also say that the one Supreme Personality supplies all the necessities of every other living creature. God is supplying food for everyone.

~ Srila Prabhupada (Science of Self Rrealization 8a: Knowing the Purpose of Life)

OPTIMISTS DO LIVE LONGER

HE SEES AN OPPORTUNITY IN EVERY CALAMITY

A PESSIMIST SEES A CALAMITY IN EVERY OPPORTUNITY

Half full or half empty? The answer could predict a person's risk of heart disease and early death.

We're told to always look on the bright side of life - and now it seems there's a good reason why.

People with a positive outlook on life are twice as likely to have healthier hearts and circulation, researchers claim.

Not only that, optimists take better care of themselves.

Compared to their more negative counterparts, they had significantly better blood sugar, healthier cholesterol readings and were more physically active.

They were also more likely to have a healthier body mass index and less likely to smoke.

The researchers, from the University of Illinois, suggested boosting people's mental well being could help tackle poor health.

A person is at risk of heart disease if they have high blood pressure, smoke, have high blood cholesterol, are diabetic, do not exercise, are overweight or obese or have a family history of heart disease.

Rosalba Hernandez, professor of social work, said: 'Individuals with the highest levels of optimism have twice the odds of being in ideal cardiovascular health compared to their more pessimistic counterparts.'

'This association remains significant, even after adjusting for socio-demographic characteristics and poor mental health.'

The study published in the journal Health Behavior and Policy Review was the first to examine associations between optimism and heart health in more than 5,000 US adults.

> Dear Optimist,
> Pessimist, and
> Realist,
>
> While you guys
> were busy arguing
> about the glass of
> water, I drank it!
>
> Sincerely,
> The Opportunist

Their heart health was measured and scored as poor, intermediate and ideal.

The scoring was based on their blood pressure, body mass index, blood sugar readings, cholesterol levels, diet, physical activity and whether they used tobacco.

They were also quizzed on their outlook on life and physical health, with researchers asking if they suffered from arthritis, liver and kidney disease.

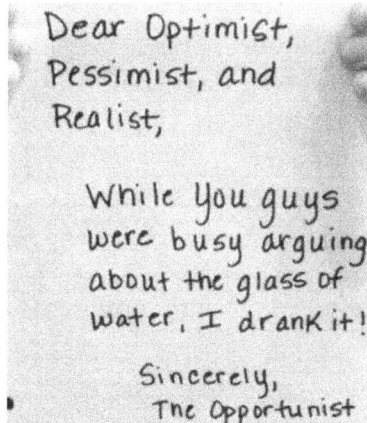

People who were the most optimistic were 50 and 76 per cent more likely to have total health scores in the intermediate or ideal ranges, respectively.

The association between optimism and cardiovascular health was even stronger when socio-demographic characteristics such as age, race and ethnicity, income and education status were factored in.

People who were the most optimistic were twice as likely to have ideal heart health, and 55 per cent more likely to have a total health score in the intermediate range.

Professor Hernandez said: 'At the population level, even this moderate difference in cardiovascular health translates into a significant reduction in death rates.'

The study backs up previous findings about the health benefits of being an optimist.

Researchers at University of Pittsburgh found women who were optimistic were 14 per cent less likely to die from any cause than pessimists.

They were also 30 per cent less likely to die from heart disease after eight years of follow up in the study.

Optimists also were also less likely to have high blood pressure, diabetes or smoke cigarettes.

But don't overdo it: One researcher believes a 'realistic sense of optimism' is key.

Sophie Chou, an organisational psychology researcher at National Taiwan University, claims people with this mindset are more likely to be happy and successful than those who are pessimistic or wildly optimistic.

A realistic optimist is defined as someone who looks on the bright side of life but has a realistic grasp on the present and what to expect in life.

She said realistic optimists use their realism to perform well at work and in exams, while their positive outlook enables them to dodge periods of depression and helps them spot opportunities.

Reference

Anna Hodgekiss, The Daily Mail, 14 January 2015

By Coco Ballantyne, Do optimists live longer? Scientific American, March 6, 2009

Doris May Lessing, Through the Tunnel, Creative Education, Inc., 1990

Sarah Kliff, Washington Post, March 1, 2013

MIND OVER MATTER?

YOU CAN IMPACT YOUR BODY WITH THOUGHT CONTROL

Anthony Robbin's Unlimited Power describes a case of a psychiatric patient with a split personality. One of her personalities was diabetic, while another was not. Her blood sugars would be normal when she was in her non-diabetic personality, but then when she shifted into her diabetic alter ego, her blood sugars rose, and all medical evidence demonstrated that she was diabetic.

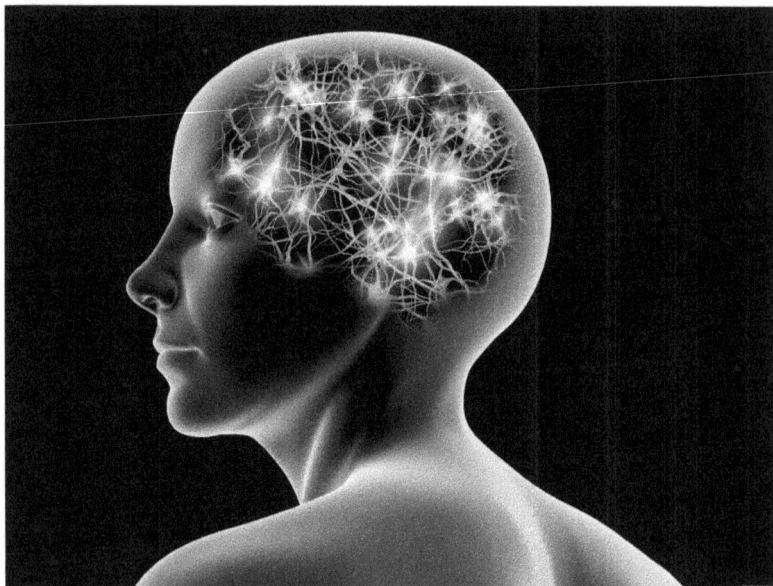

When her personality flipped back to the non-diabetic counterpart, her blood sugars normalized.

Psychiatrist Bennett Braun, author of The Treatment of Multiple Personality Disorder, describes the case of Timmy, who also had multiple personalities. One personality was allergic to orange juice, and when this personality drank orange juice, Timmy would break into blistering hives. However, another personality drinks orange juice uneventfully. If the allergic personality was in the midst of an allergy attack and he shifted back to the non-allergic personality, the hives would disappear instantly.

Reference

Stories That Will Make You Believe In the Power of Your Mind To Heal You By Lissa Rankin, MD, November, 2013

Joseph Murphy, The Power of Your Subconscious Mind, Courier Corporation

> The symptoms of the mind are determination and rejection, which are due to different kinds of desires. We desire that which is favorable to our sense gratification, and we reject that which is not favorable to sense gratification. The material mind is not fixed, but the very same mind can be fixed when engaged in the activities of Krsna consciousness. Otherwise, as long as the mind is on the material platform, it is hovering, and all this rejection and acceptance is asat, temporary.
> ~ Srimad Bhagavatam (Srimad Bhagavatam 3.26.27)

BAREFOOT TO AMERICA

I announced to my village that I was going to walk to America on the following Tuesday--October 14, 1958. No one in the village knew where America was. Then I came home and said to my mother, "Mother, I want to go to America to go to college. Will you give me your permission?" "Very well," she said. "You may go. When will you leave?" I did not want to give her time to discover how far away America was, for fear that she would change her mind. "Tomorrow," I said. "1 will prepare some maize for you to eat along the way," she said. She sent me off with enough flour for a five-day journey.

Next day I left my home in Nyasaland, East Africa. I had only the clothes I wore, a khaki shirt and shorts. I carried the two treasures I owned: a Bible and a copy of Pilgrim's Progress. I carried, too, the maize my mother had given me, wrapped in banana leaves

My goal was a continent and an ocean away, but I did not doubt that I would reach it. I had no idea how old I was. Such things mean

little in a land where time is always the same. I suppose I was 16 or 18. My father died when I was very young. From missionaries I learned I was not the victim of circumstances but the master of them. I learned that I had an obligation to use whatever talents I had to make life better for others. And to do that I would need education. I learned about America. I read the life of Abraham Lincoln and grew to love this man who suffered so much to help the enslaved in his country. I read, too, the autobiography of Booker T. Washington, himself born in slavery in America, and who had risen in dignity and honour to become a benefactor of his people and his country. I gradually realized that in America I could receive the training and opportunities to prepare myself to emulate these men in my own land, to be, like them, a leader, perhaps even the president of my country.

My intention was to make my way to Cairo, where I hoped to get passage on a ship to America. Cairo was over 3,000 miles away, a distance I could not comprehend, and I foolishly thought I could walk it in four or five days. But in four or five days I was about 25 miles from home, my food was gone, I had no money, and I did not know what to do, except that I must keep going. I developed a pattern of travel that became my life for more than a year. Villages were usually five or six miles apart, on forest paths. I would arrive at one in the afternoon and ask if I could work to earn food, water and a place to sleep. When this was possible, 1 would spend the night there, then move on to the next village in the morning. I was actually defenceless against the forest animals I dreaded, but although I heard them at night none of them approached me. Malaria mosquitoes, however, were constant companions, and I often was sick.

By the end of a year I had walked 1,000 miles and had arrived in Uganda, where a family took me in and I found a job making bricks. I remained there six months and sent most of my earnings to my mother. In Kampala, I unexpectedly came upon a directory of American colleges. Opening it at random, I saw the name of Skagit Valley College, Mount Vernon, Washington. I had heard that American colleges sometimes give scholarships to deserving young people, so I wrote and applied for one. I realized that I might be refused but was not discouraged; I would write to one school after another in the directory until I found one that would help me.

Three weeks later I was granted a scholarship and assured that the school would help me find a job. Overjoyed, I went to the United States authorities, only to be told that this was not enough. I would need a passport and the round-trip fare in order to obtain a visa. I wrote to my government for a passport but it was refused because I could not tell them when I was born. I then wrote to the missionaries who had taught me in my childhood, and through their efforts was granted a passport. But I still could not get the visa because I did not have the fare. Still determined, I resumed my journey. So strong was my faith that I used my last money to buy my first pair of shoes; I knew I could not walk into college in my bare feet. I carried the shoes to save them.

Across Uganda and into the Sudan I walked. The villages were

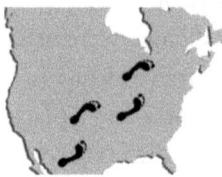

farther apart and the people were less friendly. Sometimes I had to walk 20 or 30 miles in a day to find a place to sleep or to work to earn some food. When I ran out of food, I drank sugar water.

At last I reached Khartoum, where I learned that there was a United States consulate. Once again I heard about the US entrance requirements, but this time the Consul was interested enough to write to the college about my plight. Back came a cable. The students, hearing about me and my problems, had raised the fare of $1,700 through benefit parties. I was thrilled and deeply grateful, - overjoyed that I had judged Americans correctly for their friendship and brotherhood. News that I had walked for over two years and 2,500 miles circulated in Khartoum.

After many, many months, carrying my two books and wearing my first suit, I arrived at Skagit Valley College. In my speech of gratitude to the student body I disclosed my desire to become prime minister or president of my country, and I noticed some smiles. I wondered if I had said something naive. I do not think so. When God has put an impossible dream in your heart, He means to help you fulfil it. I believed this to be true when as an African bush boy, I felt compelled to become an American college graduate. And my dream of becoming president of my country can also become true."

(From Legson Kyira's Autobiography - I Will Try)

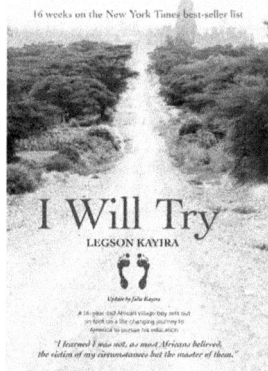

Just like suppose I came to your country, United States of America. Oh, in my childhood I heard of it in school when I was reading history or geography. I heard first of all. I did not come first of all. So hearing, hearing, when I understood, "Oh, that's a very wonderful country, and it is far away, and I should go there..." Similarly, as you think also about going to India, so first of all hearing. Not immediately seeing what is America or what is India. First of all hearing. So similarly, if we want to see God, then we have to hear. That is the process. In Krsna consciousness process, the first step is hearing. Sravanam. Sravanam means hearing.

~ Srila Prabhupada (Lecture, Bhagavad-gita 4.34 -- New York, August 14, 1966)

A TRANSCENDENTAL JOURNEY TO AMERICA

AN EXTRAORDINARY TALE OF BOUNDLESS COURAGE AND AN UNFAILING DETERMINATION

It was Friday, August 13th, 1965. At 9.00 in the morning, a lonely, elderly gentleman, A.C.Bhaktivedanta Swami boards a ship at Calcutta port, sailing to New York. The black cargo ship, small and weathered was anchored at dock side. Sailors curiously saw the elderly saffron dressed Sadhu, as he spoke last words to his companion in the taxi and walked determinedly towards the boat.

He had only a suitcase, an umbrella and a supply of dry cereal as hand baggage. There was no one on the shore to bid him good bye, no friends, no supporters, no disciples.

He was going to America to preach Krishna bhakti, which had been known only in India. What follows is a remarkable tale of faith and determination, beyond anyone's imagination.

He carried with him 40 rupees, he had no institutional backing, no support awaited him. He was going on the order of his spiritual master to teach Krishna consciousness to the English speaking world. He was carrying the almost forgotten spiritual culture of Vedic India to plant it in the heart of America's cultural turmoil of 1960s.

But such a voyage was not an easy one for some one aged 69. The ensuing journey presented considerable hardships. On board the ship,

Srila Prabhupada wrote of sea sickness, dizziness, vomiting, heavy rains in Bay of Bengal.

On the 13th day of the voyage, during the passage through the Arabian sea, he suffered a massive heart attack. All alone, helpless and without medical assistance, in his uneasy sleep that night he had a dream, a vision. Lord Krishna appeared and took charge of the ship, along with his other incarnations. Krishna was smiling at Srila Prabhupada and was pulling the ship all the way to America.

After crossing the Meditaranean Sea, the ship came into the Atlantic Ocean but the ocean became like a placid lake. The captain said that never in his career, had he seen such a calm Atlantic crossing. The captain's wife asked Srila Prabhupada to come back with them so that they might have another such sailing.

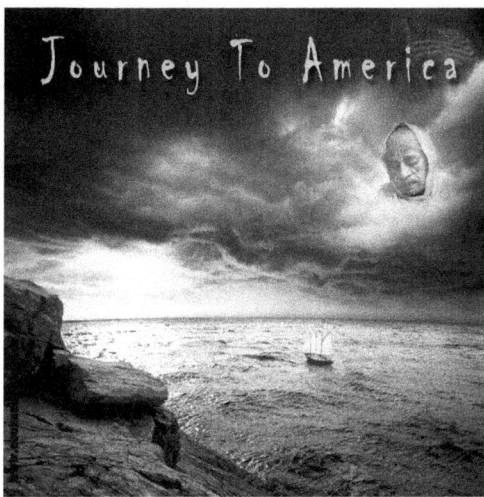

Srila Prabhupada wrote in his diary, "If the Atlantic would have shown its usual face, I would have died but Lord Krishna has taken charge of the ship."

You once gave the measure for becoming a successful preacher: "One must have the courage of an Englishman and the heart of a Bengali mother." Certainly your life is the full embodiment of this standard.

As for courage, on a morning walk in Calcutta you were reminiscing about your childhood days. You described how you climbed up the scaffolding to the top of the Victoria Memorial. A devotee remarked, "Srila Prabhupada, you must have been very brave." You countered, "And I am still brave! Otherwise, how have I come to the West all alone?"

~ From a Vyasa Puja offering

111

On September 17th, 1965, the ship arrived at Boston's Commonwealth Pier. Seeing the Boston skyline and rampant materialism prevalent in the lives of the people there, Srila Prabhupada realized the difficulties in his mission. He saw the hellish city life, people dedicated to the illusory material happiness. He felt weak, lowly and unable to help them on his own. He was penniless, he had barely survived two heart attacks at sea, he spoke a different language. He dressed strangely according to American standards and he had come to tell people to give up sinful habits which were inseparable part of their lives. He had come to teach Americans worship of Lord Krishna who to them was a mythical Hindu God. What would he be able to accomplish? Helplessly he spoke his heart to Lord Krishna in a famous poem, 'markine bhgavat dharma', preaching Bhagavad dharma in America.

After a total of 38 days, the ship at last arrived at New York where Srila Prabhupada disembarked onto a lonely Brooklyn Pier, not knowing whether to turn left or right, to begin his mission in the West.

Srila Prabhupada's voyage on the ship name Jaladuta 50 years ago, marked the beginning of a spiritual revival and the 12 years after his arrival in America saw the Hare Krishna movement spread to major cities worldwide.

For thousands of years, the Vedic tradition had been confined to the boundaries of India. To a world immersed in materialistic ethos,

---

Impossible Is A Word Found In A Fool's Dictionary
The story of the printing of Caitanya-caritamrta by Srila Prabhupada's disciples (described in Srila Prabhupada Lilamrta, Volume 6) serves as a striking illustration. When Srila Prabhupada ordered his disciples at the Bhaktivedanta Book Trust to print seventeen books in two months, they initially replied that it was an impossible task. Srila Prabhupada chided, "Impossible is a word found in a fool's dictionary." So they set to work, fully enlivened by the powerful order of their spiritual master. When the huge task was completed in the allotted time, everyone knew that both the order and its execution were the causeless mercy of Krsna's pure devotee.

Srila Prabhupada revealed the wisdom of this timeless philosophy of Krishna consciousness.

SRILA PRABHUPADA'S LEGACY

He observed his 70th birthday in the ship. In 1965, when he first arrived by freighter in New York City, Srila Prabhupada was practically penniless. It was after almost a year of great difficulty that he established the International Society for Krishna Consciousness in July of 1966. Under his careful guidance, the Society grew within a decade to a worldwide confederation of almost one hundred asramas, schools, temples, institutes and farm communities.

In the eleven years that followed his arrival in America, Srila Prabhupada circled the globe 14 times on lecture tours, bringing the teachings of Lord Krishna to thousands of people on six continents. Srila Prabhupada also established what would become the world's largest vegetarian food relief program. With the desire to nourish the roots of Krishna consciousness in its home, Srila Prabhupada returned to India several times, where he sparked a revival in the Vaishnava tradition. In India, he opened dozens of temples, including large centers in the holy towns of Vrindavan and Mayapur.

In 1968, Srila Prabhupada created New Vrndavana, an experimental Vedic community in the hills of West Virginia. Inspired

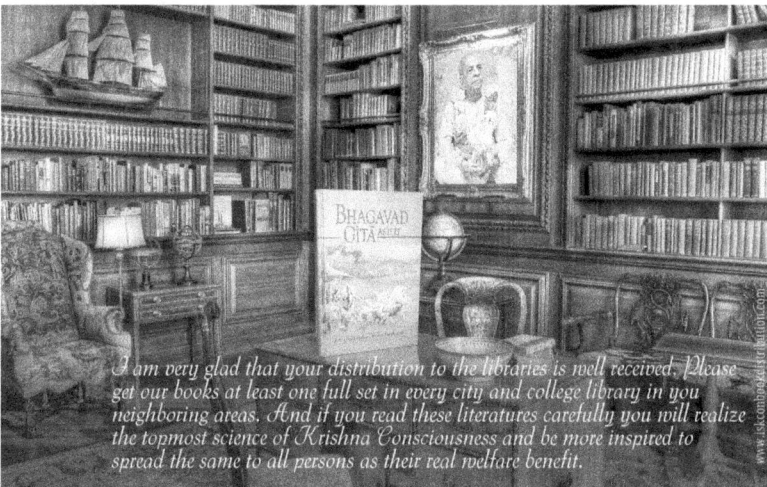

I am very glad that your distribution to the libraries is well received. Please get our books at least one full set in every city and college library in you neighboring areas. And if you read these literatures carefully you will realize the topmost science of Krishna Consciousness and be more inspired to spread the same to all persons as their real welfare benefit.

by the success of New Vrndavana, now a thriving farm community of more than one thousand acres, his students have since founded several similar communities in the United States and abroad.

In 1972, His Divine Grace introduced the Vedic system of primary and secondary education in the West by founding the Gurukula school in Dallas, Texas.

Srila Prabhupada's most significant contribution, however, is his books. Highly respected by scholars for their authority, depth, and clarity, they are used as textbooks in numerous college courses. He authored over 90 volumes on Vedic philosophy and his writings have been translated into over 100 languages. More than a billion copies of his books have been sold so far. His most prominent works include: Bhagavad-gita As It Is, the 30-volume Srimad-Bhagavatam, and the 17-volume Sri Caitanya-caritamrita. His writings constitute a veritable library of Vedic philosophy, religion, literature and culture.

The Bhaktivedanta Book Trust, established in 1972 exclusively to publish the works of His Divine Grace, has become the world's largest publisher of books in the field of Indian religion and philosophy.

Reference
Srila Prabhupada Lilamrta, Vol.1, Satsvarupa dasa Goswami, BBTI

THE AUTHOR

Dr. Sahadeva dasa (Sanjay Shah) is a monk in vaisnava tradition. His areas of work include research in Vedic and contemporary thought, Corporate and educational training, social work and counselling, travelling, writing books and of course, practicing spiritual life and spreading awareness about the same.

He is also an accomplished musician, composer, singer, instruments player and sound engineer. He has more than a dozen albums to his credit so far. (SoulMelodies.com) His varied interests include alternative holistic living, Vedic studies, social criticism, environment, linguistics, history, art & crafts, nature studies, web technologies etc.

Many of his books have been acclaimed internationally and translated in other languages.

By The Same Author

Oil-Final Countdown To A Global Crisis And Its Solutions
End of Modern Civilization And Alternative Future
To Kill Cow Means To End Human Civilization
Cow And Humanity - Made For Each Other
Cows Are Cool - Love 'Em!
Let's Be Friends - A Curious, Calm Cow
Wondrous Glories of Vraja
We Feel Just Like You Do
Tsunami Of Diseases Headed Our Way - Know Your Food Before Time Runs Out
Cow Killing And Beef Export - The Master Plan To Turn India Into A Desert
Capitalism Communism And Cowism - A New Economics For The 21st Century
Noble Cow - Munching Grass, Looking Curious And Just Hanging Around
World - Through The Eyes Of Scriptures
To Save Time Is To Lengthen Life
Life Is Nothing But Time - Time Is Life, Life Is Time
Lost Time Is Never Found Again
Spare Us Some Carcasses - An Appeal From The Vultures
An Inch of Time Can Not Be Bought With A Mile of Gold
Cow Dung For Food Security And Survival of Human Race
Cow Dung – A Down To Earth Solution To Global Warming And Climate Change
Career Women - The Violence of Modern Jobs And The Lost Art of Home Making
Working Moms And Rise of A Lost Generation
Glories of Thy Wondrous Name
India A World Leader in Cow Killing And Beef Export - An Italian Did It In 10 Years
As Long As There Are Slaughterhouses, There Will Be Wars
Peak Soil – Industrial Civilization, On The Verge of Eating Itself
If Violence Must Stop, Slaughterhouses Must Close Down
Corporatocracy - You Are A Corporate Citizen, A Slave of Invisible And Ruthless Masters
(More information on availability on DrDasa.com)

www.ingramcontent.com/pod-product-compliance
Lightning Source LLC
Chambersburg PA
CBHW070639030426
42337CB00020B/4082